Storytelling with Puppets, Props, and Playful Tales

by Mary Jo Huff

Publisher: Roberta Suid
Copy Editor: Carol Whiteley
Cover Design and Production: Scott McMorrow
Cover Photograph: Bill Smith

Also by the author: *Storytellin' Time* video (MM 2062).

ISBN 1-57612-042-2

Printed in the United States of America

987654321

CONTENTS

My personal thanks...

To all the children whose eyes have lit up when they listened to a story, especially my grandchildren Kurt, Melanie, Matthew, and Michael. To my family—Cathy, Joe, Melody, Kenny, John, and Nikki, who have always encouraged this endeavor; especially my husband Bill, who has endured the daily hardships of my organized chaos; my mom, who never knows what to expect next; and my dad, who had a real gift for gab.

To the members of Friends of Storytelling. To my road partners, Sharon Hall and Carol Rogers, for their patient listening and their advice over the years. To my sister, Connie Elbrink, who teaches third grade and invited me to stop by and tell a story any time. To my puppet connection, Joyce Davis, who keeps her best friend in a basket. To my writing angels, Lucille VanWinkle and Christine Kallevig. To Maria Elena Buria, Billy's mama. To my USI connections: Dr. Sheri Boyd; Barbara Plum, a wonderful lady and friend who loved children; and the teachers, parents, and children of Kinder Kountry Pre-School for the years of fun and support.

There is no better way to share life than with a group of children and a good story. To each of you who values the art of storytelling and enjoys this book I say, "Hand down the past to the present and preserve the present for the future. Tell a story!"

INTRODUCTION

In today's modern world, storytelling has become a lost art. Paper and pen, the typewriter, and now the computer have replaced the oral story sharing that was once the way to keep our cultures and heritage alive.

But things are changing. The ancient art of storytelling is being resurrected to once again play an important role within families and as part of school curriculums. As an early childhood educator for 24 years and a professional storyteller for 6, I am very happy to see this new interest. And since I believe that everyone is a storyteller, I have written *Storytelling with Puppets, Props, and Playful Tales* to motivate you to find the storyteller within yourself and to become creative and comfortable telling stories to young children.

Storytelling with Puppets, Props, and Playful Tales is appropriate for children of all ages. Working with the ideas found in this book will help you to:
- stimulate imaginations
- develop oral communication skills
- increase auditory discrimination
- strengthen listening and pre-reading skills
- encourage creativity
- improve fine motor skills
- promote visual discrimination
- develop critical thinking skills
- strengthen sequencing skills
- encourage participation
- create a love of books, reading, and, eventually, writing

The book is divided into three parts: "Puppets and Playful Tales," "Props and Playful Tales," and "Story Corners and Playful Tales." Storytelling techniques for the non-professional storyteller will be introduced, as well as how to make and use storytelling puppets and props and how to put together an exciting storytelling corner. Tales and chants to use with the storytelling aids are also included.

Storytelling with Puppets, Props, and Playful Tales was written with you in mind. I encourage you to take from this book storytelling ideas that are a part of my life and share them with a child. There are new and exciting story experiences waiting for you just around the corner.

TIPS FOR TELLING STORIES

Discover the right story to tell:
- Look for stories that are age appropriate.
- Find stories that you love and believe in.
- Check picture books written for different age levels.
- Collect stories from family, friends, and community.
- Create your own stories.

Learn the story:
- By reading it several times.
- By breaking it into a beginning, middle, and end.

Retell the story many times:
- Listen to yourself telling the story.
- Tape-record your version.
- Practice telling the story to family and friends.

Speak naturally:
- Use your normal speaking voice.
- Use sound effects, such as unusual voice and story sounds, sparingly.

Use simple, natural gestures:
- Add gestures when they add to the story, but don't overuse them.

Polish the story:
- By telling it, retelling it, and retelling it.

Once you have a story ready to tell, create a story corner in which to tell it. You can set one up with the story corner props described in "Story Corners and Playful Tales." Then . . . BEGIN!

Make eye contact with your listeners.
Introduce the story.
Tell the story looking directly into your listeners' eyes.
Encourage your listeners to interact with you.
Enjoy and work with your audience's enthusiasm.

DEVELOPING A STORYTELLING CURRICULUM

To make the most of storytelling's benefits, stories need to be repeated again and again. If you use a literature-based curriculum, you'll be able to extend a story's ideas throughout the day. As you do, listen for the children to retell the story in their own special way.

The following is just a sample of how a story can be extended using "The Farmer's Headache." I encourage you to adapt these possibilities to suit your curriculum.

Story talk. Ask the children if they have ever had a headache or if someone they know has complained of a headache. Does noise bother a person with a headache? What remedy is there for a headache? Why did the farmer have a headache?

Art. The children can create stick puppets for the characters in the story and add more characters to the plot. Set out scissors, markers, construction paper, tagboard, laminated paper, glue, and Popsicle sticks. Several types of paper provide different textures for the puppets.

Cooking. Bake animal-shaped sugar cookies and let the children retell the story during snack time.

Story corner. To help children retell the story, provide storytelling materials in a story corner. You can create a farm yard story box by cutting slits in a box top and placing stick puppets in the slits as the story unfolds. Puppets with magnets can be used on a magnetic board and story board characters can be attached to a board with Velcro pieces. Supply the corner with plenty of books about farmers and have paper, pencils, markers, crayons, and scissors available for children to create their own characters for storytelling.

Math. Have the children count the animals annoying the farmer. Let each child choose a favorite animal and then graph the results. The children can also predict and then graph which animal made the loudest noise.

Science. Play a tape of different animal sounds and let the children identify the animals. Which animal has the loudest sound and which one has the softest? What do the animals eat? Do they live inside or outside the barn? Talk about the different sounds that children hear daily.

STORY CLASSIFICATIONS

Storytelling with puppets and props isn't limited to just one kind of story. When you develop your storytelling curriculum, be sure to include a good variety of story types:

Fables—Short tales that have a moral and communicate a truth about life. The main characters in fables are often animals that act and think like humans.

Fairy tales—Stories that often feature fairies, elves, genies, pixies, leprechauns, and other make-believe characters.

Legends—Stories that revolve around incidents that are believed to have taken place in a particular culture's history.

Folk tales—Stories that come to us from many parts of the world. These stories reflect a particular country or people's flavor and preserve cultural traditions.

Poetry—Rhyming poetry, in particular Mother Goose rhymes, is a source of excellent stories for young children.

PUPPET AND PROP MATERIALS

Most of the materials needed for puppet and prop making are readily available and inexpensive to purchase in craft, discount, grocery, or teacher supply stores. Some of the items, such as shoe boxes, old gloves or socks, and toilet tissue rolls, the children can bring from home. Construction materials for making a portable story wall will cost a bit more, but the wall will be usable for years to come.

One material that is used often in puppet and prop making and in the story corner is Velcro. To be effective, the soft side, or "loop" side, of a piece of Velcro must meet the rougher side, or the "hook" side, of another piece of Velcro. Be sure when making puppets or props to use with a Velcro story board, story can, or other storytelling accessory that the Velcro on the puppet will adhere to the Velcro on the story board. Self-adhesive hook Velcro can be cut into small pieces that you store till needed in a plastic bag. Self-adhesive Velcro can be placed on art foam, poster board, laminated materials, plastic, wood, felt, and fabric; it can also be applied to felt-board characters you already have so that you can use them with the Velcro boards detailed in this book. If Velcro pieces do not stick well, add a drop of quick-bonding glue and press in place. When disengaging puppets or props that have been attached to a surface with Velcro, place your thumb at the top of the item and gently pull down.

THE BENEFITS OF STORYTELLING

PUPPETS

Puppets are a powerful way to reach children—even the shy child will relate to a puppet. Puppets are also multisensory vehicles for storytelling, and create an art and language experience that children can understand. When you find a special puppet, and give it a personality and a home, you'll be amazed how children interact with it. Use it in your story corner and throughout your curriculum.

PROPS

Going beyond simply reading a story adds a great deal to the reading/listening experience. Using props:
- Creates story awareness.
- Helps the children to hear and feel the language.
- Makes each story come alive.
- Lets the children participate in the story and develop fine motor skills as they manipulate props and puppets.
- Helps the children learn to retell stories.

STORY CORNERS

Storytelling involves cooperation and interaction. This in turn promotes literacy and love of language. Encourage the children to interact during your storytelling. Also encourage parents to tell family and other stories to the children. Experience with interactive storytelling will provide a solid foundation on which to build future reading and writing skills.

PART I

PUPPETS AND PLAYFUL TALES

STORYTELLING WITH PUPPETS

THE PUPPETEER

Find a story with one or two main characters—this will help since you have only two hands for holding puppets! If a story has many characters, let the children act out the smaller parts.

When you tell the story, give your puppet a special voice and character. Puppets are magical, and the audience should focus on the puppet and not the puppeteer. Find a comfort zone with your puppet and story. Children never get tired of hearing or acting out favorites, such as "The Three Bears" and "The Three Little Pigs." Treat the puppets as if they were alive. But also remember that some children are not used to puppets. Proceed with caution.

PUPPET VOICES

Once you've created a puppet, spend some time with it to learn its character. Experiment with your voice to decide what the puppet's voice should be. Using a lower pitch is easier at the beginning. Work up to a higher pitch to give yourself a three-level range: normal, high, and low. Once your puppet has its own voice, you are ready to tell the story. Puppets with open mouths are more expressive.

PUPPET ETIQUETTE

Puppets should never be allowed to fight. Many times children try to make puppets bite, punch, or hit each other. Give direction on how they are to use their puppets. Set limits for puppet activity and treat the puppets with respect. The children will model your behavior.

PUPPET HOUSES

Give your puppets a place to live. Also be sure puppets have a special place to enter the story. Do not let the audience see you put on a puppet or take one off your hand.

MASCOT

Giving the story corner a mascot—complete with name, voice, and personality—will help children relate to puppet storytelling. Keep the mascot puppet in a special house and bring it to life to prepare the children for circle time, story time, or as a transition tool.

INTRODUCING THE PUPPETS

Use a soft voice at first and gradually change it as needed in the story. Move the puppet slowly. Touch the puppet gently, and let it whisper in your ear or in each child's ear. Let all the children touch the puppet. Ask the children if they want the puppet to help tell a story. Provide puppets for the children to use on their own.

BOX PUPPET

The great thing about the box puppet is that it's easy to put together. The directions are for creating a frog puppet, but different colors of paint and different types of boxes will let children produce box puppets for story characters.

MATERIALS
2 empty Jell-O boxes, scissors, heavy cloth tape or duct tape, glue, brown and green paint, sponges, brush, plastic eyes, pipe cleaners or crinkled paper

DIRECTIONS
Open one end of each of the Jell-O boxes. Cut off three of the end flaps on each box, retaining one of the long flaps. Place the boxes side by side and tape the two flaps together with heavy tape. Paint the boxes green for a frog puppet. Then sponge paint over the base color different shades of brown and green. Glue on eyes and pipe cleaner or paper legs (see the illustration). Adults can work the puppet's mouth by putting a thumb in the bottom box and four fingers in the top box, but children may find it easier to put one hand in each box.

STORY RETELLING
Let each child use a frog puppet to retell the tale "Down by the Pond" (see p. 38). The children can use the frogs to answer questions about the pond and take them home to use for retelling the story to their families. Keep a frog box puppet in the story corner for the children to use.

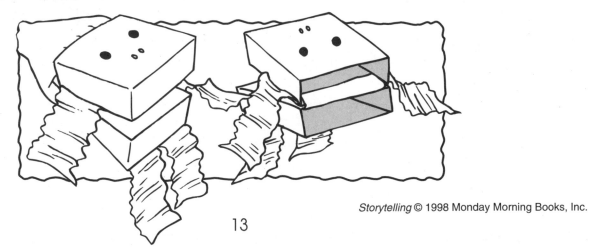

Storytelling © 1998 Monday Morning Books, Inc.

FINGER PUPPET

Finger puppets are designed to fit on the fingers or thumb. They are small enough to fit in a shirt pocket, clear pencil case or VCR tape box, small bag, or apron pocket; they are also easy to make and store. The following directions are for a generic puppet that you and the children can decorate to fit any story.

MATERIALS
Glove fingers
Velcro fabric
Heavy felt
Needle and thread
Upholstery fabric
Glue
Scissors
Quilt batting or cotton
Decorative materials

DIRECTIONS
Cut out fingers of a glove.
Glue or sew decorative items to the fingers.
If the puppet is larger than a child's finger, stuff it with a small amount of batting or cotton.
To use the finger puppet with a Velcro story board, attach a piece of Velcro hook.

Finger puppets can be stored in clear, labeled VCR tape holders. The children will learn to recognize the labels and find their favorite story characters.

STORY RETELLING
Create a set of finger puppets to use with stories during the year. Place the puppets in the story corner so the children can retell their favorite story or make one up.

FINGER PUPPET PLAYHOUSE

This playhouse will accommodate many finger puppets—an entire family could live here!

MATERIALS
Large cereal box, spray paint, craft knife, permanent markers

DIRECTIONS
Spray paint a wide, tall cereal box. Cut out windows and a door for the puppets to use. Cut a large hole in the back of the box for the children to put their hands through. Use permanent markers to outline where the windows and door are on the back of the box so the storyteller can tell the story and move the puppets more easily. The finger puppets can be stored in the bottom of the box. A town can be created with several boxes and puppets for the houses.

STORY RETELLING
The children can use the playhouse and finger puppets for neighborhood conversations and storytelling from one house to another. Provide several houses in the story corner and rotate the puppets to develop the children's imaginations.

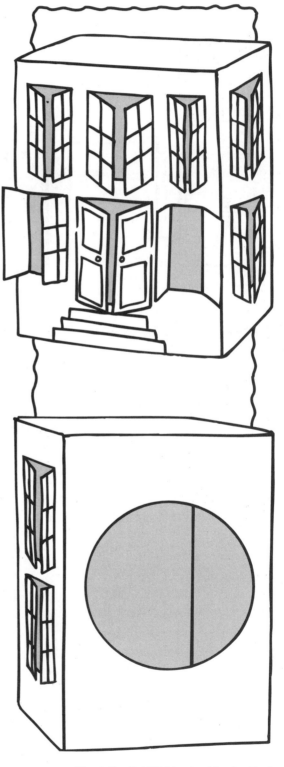

Storytelling © 1998 Monday Morning Books, Inc.

FINGER PUPPET PLAYHOUSE

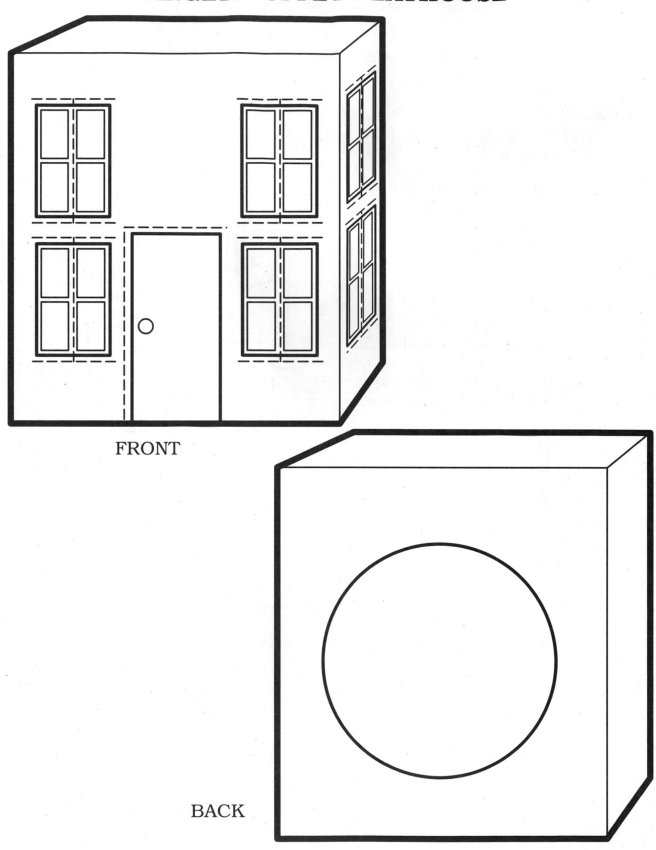

FRONT

BACK

FOLDED PAPER PUPPET

Use folded construction to create a fierce "talking" alligator.

MATERIALS
Heavy construction paper or tagboard in several colors (9" x 12" (23 cm x 30 cm) will make a child-size puppet; 12" x 18" (30 cm x 46 cm) is better for an adult-sized puppet), markers, glue, scissors, decorative materials (feathers, buttons, plastic eyes, etc.)

DIRECTIONS
Fold the construction paper lengthwise into three equal parts.

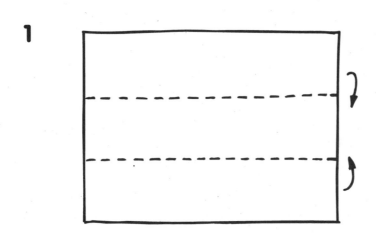

Storytelling © 1998 Monday Morning Books, Inc.

With the open side down on the table, fold in half.

2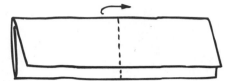

Fold the top and bottom back to meet in the middle. The open flap is on the inside.

3 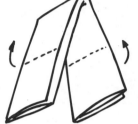 **4**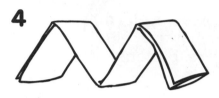

Add eyes to distinguish the top of the puppet. In the illustration, white circles and black circles are glued on to create large alligator eyes. White paper zigzag teeth are glued to the open area to create a fierce alligator mouth.

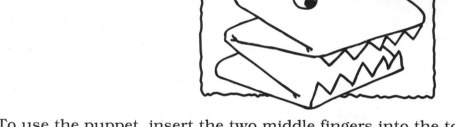

To use the puppet, insert the two middle fingers into the top opening. Keep the index and pinky for balance on the outside. Putting the thumb into the bottom opening gets you ready to make your puppet talk.

STORY RETELLING

The puppet shown here can be used to retell the story "Mr. Alligator and the Monkeys" (see p. 19). Children can also construct their own story characters to use with other tales or with one they create. After a story has been chosen and a puppet has been made, send home a note to the parents announcing that their child has a special story to tell or retell. This kind of activity will let parents share part of their child's day.

MR. ALLIGATOR
AND THE MONKEYS TALE

Five little monkeys swinging in a tree,
Teasing Mr. Alligator—"You can't catch me!" (high-pitched voice)
Along came Mr. Alligator—
Sluuuuuuurrrrrrpppppppp!

Four little monkeys swinging in a tree,
Teasing Mr. Alligator—"You can't catch me!"
Along came Mr. Alligator—
Sluuuuuuurrrrrrpppppppp!

Three little monkeys swinging in a tree,
Teasing Mr. Alligator—"You can't catch me!"
Along came Mr. Alligator—
Sluuuuuuurrrrrrpppppppp!

Two little monkeys swinging in a tree,
Teasing Mr. Alligator—"You can't catch me!"
Along came Mr. Alligator—
Sluuuuuuurrrrrrpppppppp!

One little monkey swinging in a tree,
Teasing Mr. Alligator—"You can't catch me!"
Along came Mr. Alligator—
Sluuuuuuurrrrrrpppppppp!

That one little monkey swung out of the tree,
And yelled, "Ha! Ha! Ha! You can't catch me!"

Storytelling © 1998 Monday Morning Books, Inc.

MR. ALLIGATOR
AND THE MONKEYS PROPS

These puppets and props can be used, along with the folded paper alligator, with a story board or story apron for the telling of "Mr. Alligator and the Monkeys."

MATERIALS
Art foam (brown and green), Velcro hook, scissors, glue

DIRECTIONS
Tree—Cut out a tree trunk shape from brown art foam and a rounded top from green art foam. Attach the top and bottom with glue. Cut out holes as indicated. Attach hook Velcro. Place on story apron (p. 104) or on story board (p. 110).

Monkeys—Cut out five monkeys from brown art foam using the patterns as a guide. Attach a small piece of Velcro hook to each raised paw. Attach the monkeys to the tree where the holes are cut out.

STORY RETELLING
Provide the children with a set of monkeys, a tree, and their own folded paper Mr. Alligator puppet. Have them retell the tale of Mr. Alligator and the five monkeys or make up their own version.

TREE PATTERN

GLOVE PUPPET

Old gloves find new life as chicken, rooster, and turkey puppets.

MATERIALS

Adult- or child-sized glove, quilt batting, dowel, string, glue, decorative materials (yarn, feathers, felt, plastic eyes, etc.)

DIRECTIONS

Stuff the glove with quilt batting. Coat one end of the dowel with a generous amount of glue and insert it into the glove. Tie a string tightly around the open end of the glove to enclose the dowel. Leaving only a short length of the dowel extending from the glove will give the puppet a neater appearance. Decorate the puppet to suit the story. This type of puppet works well as a duck, chicken, turkey, rooster, or any kind of bird.

STORY RETELLING

With a variety of glove puppets in the story corner, children can retell many different stories as well as create their own.

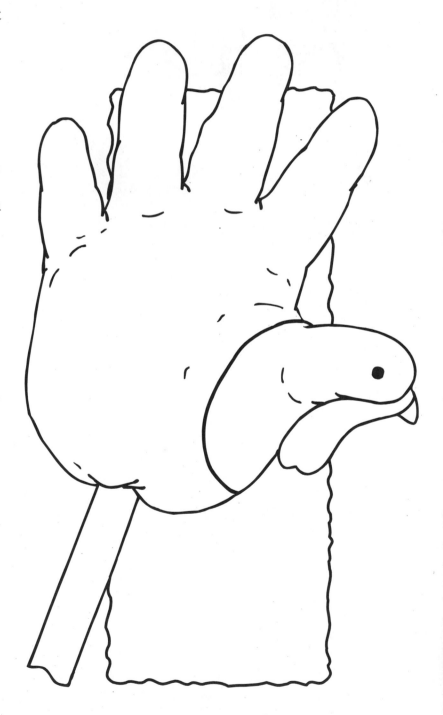

GLOVE PUPPET INTERACTIVE CHANT

Hey, Mr. Turkey! (leader)
Hey, Mr. Turkey! (child)
Hey, Mr. Turkey! (leader)
Hey, Mr. Turkey! (child)
You who! You who! (leader)

Hey, Mr. Turkey! (leader)
Hey, Mr. Turkey! (child)
Hey, Mr. Turkey! (leader)
Hey, Mr. Turkey! (child)
I'm gonna catch you! (leader)

Hey, Mr. Turkey! (leader)
Hey, Mr. Turkey! (child)
Hey, Mr. Turkey! (leader)
Hey, Mr. Turkey! (child)
Way up in that tree! (leader)

Hey, Mr. Turkey! (leader)
Hey, Mr. Turkey! (child)
Hey, Mr. Turkey! (leader)
Hey, Mr. Turkey! (child)
Fly away free! (leader)

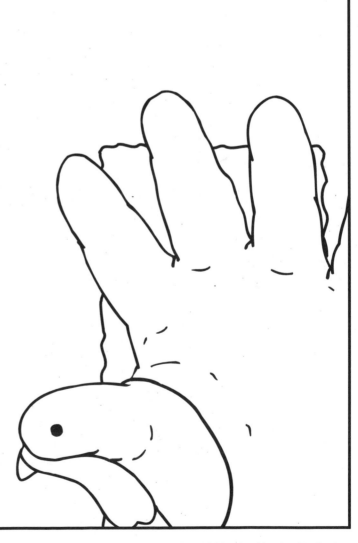

HAND PUPPET

Hand puppets can be an essential part of your curriculum and are fun for children to use. Hand puppets can be made with or without mouths, but puppets with mouths are usually preferable. The following pattern can be adapted to make people- or animal-shaped puppets. Encourage the children to use their imaginations to add faces, ears, hair, and clothes.

MATERIALS
Felt, upholstery fabric, Velcro fabric
Art foam
Laminated card stock
Glue
Needle and thread
Scissors
Other decorative materials (yarn, feathers, plastic eyes, etc.)

DIRECTIONS
Cut out two pattern shapes using the fabric you choose.
Sew or glue them together leaving the bottom open.
If you use Velcro fabric, glue or sew the wrong sides together. This fabric will not fray.
Velcro hook can be attached to decorative items to change a puppet's personality.

STORY RETELLING
This type of puppet is fun and easy for children to use. Show them how to insert their hand the first time they use one. Keep the puppets in a puppet house in the story corner for the children to use.

HAND PUPPET PATTERN

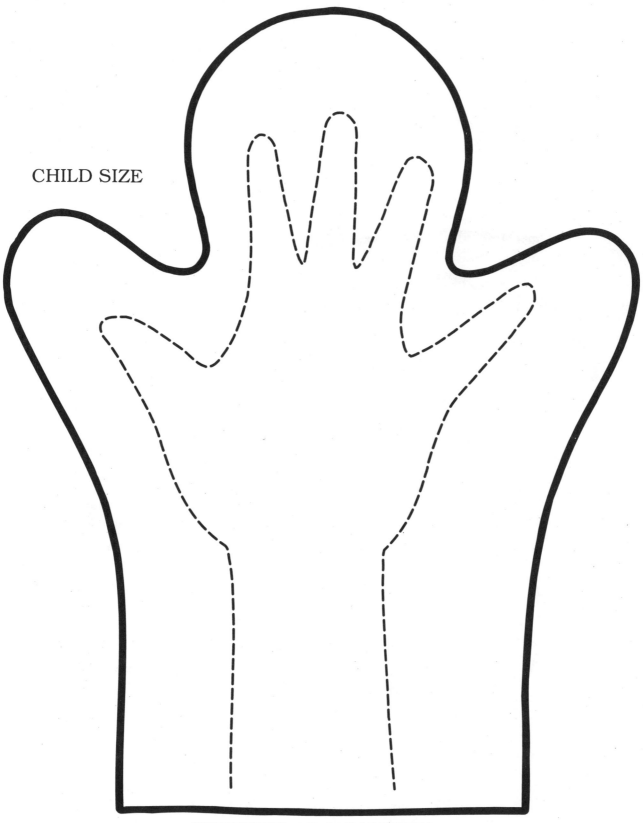

CHILD SIZE

SHORTEN OR LENGTHEN

OPEN-MOUTH "TALKING" PUPPET

A puppet that can open its mouth, talk, and even eat will be an exciting storytelling motivator. Children can turn this pattern into any number of characters.

MATERIALS

Upholstery fabric, fake fur, variety of fabrics (heavy felt or cotton fused with Pellon, denim), Velcro fabric and hook, scissors, pins, sewing machine and thread or fabric glue, decorative materials (yarn, plastic eyes, etc.)

DIRECTIONS

Cut out two puppet bodies from Velcro. This fabric will let the puppet be transformed into different characters by simply attaching different heads and tails with Velcro hook. Place the right sides of the bodies together and sew to the spot indicated in the illustration. Leave both ends open. The pattern can be extended to make a caterpillar, snake, etc.

Place the mouth pattern on the fold and cut out. Pin the mouth into place and sew it on; backstitch over the corners or use fabric glue to reinforce them. Cut a slit in the center of the mouth and stitch or glue down the material you turn under.

STORY RETELLING

Because a talking puppet can talk and eat, it should have a house and some things to munch on. Children can create these different items as well as a variety of heads and tails to use with their puppets. They will be able to use the talking puppets to tell a number of tales as well as create their own characters and stories.

Storytelling © 1998 Monday Morning Books, Inc.

BODY PATTERN

CHILD SIZE

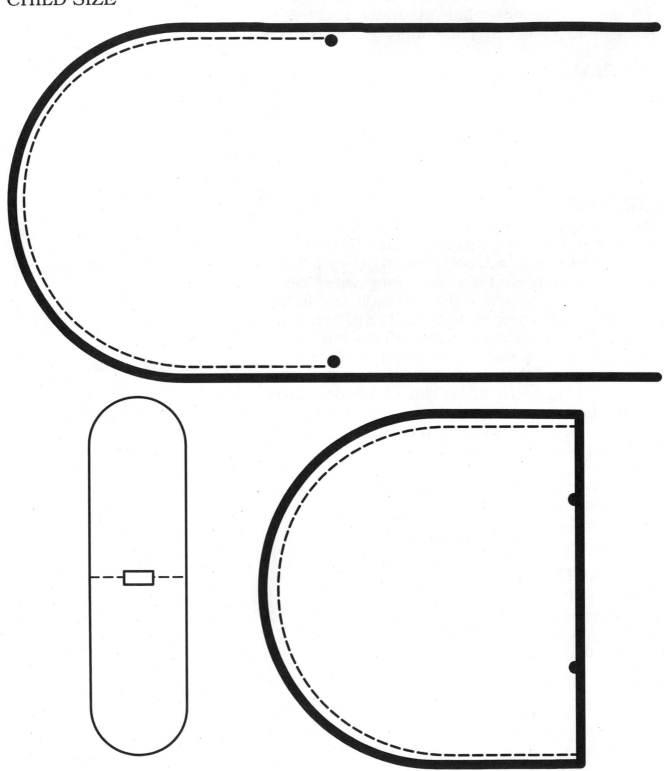

THE LION AND THE MOUSE

One day, Lion lay fast asleep in a clearing at the edge of the forest. His great mane covered his head and his head rested on his giant paws.

A timid little mouse, on his way home, came scurrying by and bumped into the great animal. Hastily he tried to run away but the lion awakened as the mouse hurried across his mane. With a loud roar Lion grabbed the little mouse in his paw and was ready to eat him.

"Please let me go, spare me!" said the mouse. "Some day I will repay you!"

With a laughing roar, the lion let the little mouse go because he had been brave enough to ask for mercy. "A brave little fellow," thought the generous lion.

Some days later, the lion was stalking his prey in the deep forest when he was caught in a hunter's net. Unable to get out, the lion roared an angry, loud roar.

The little mouse heard the roar and knew it belonged to the lion. He followed the sound of more roars and found the lion tightly trapped in the hunter's net.

"I will help you," explained the little mouse.

"How can you help me?" asked the lion. "If I cannot tear the ropes loose, no one can."

"I told you I would help you some day," said the mouse. He began to gnaw on the net. He gnawed on the net until the lion was freed.

"Now aren't you sorry you laughed at me when I said I would repay you some day?" asked the mouse. "Even a tiny little mouse can help a king like you."

Storytelling © 1998 Monday Morning Books, Inc.

LION PATTERN

Use the body pattern with these lion and mouse puppets.

LION—Cut out the lion's head and add curly yarn to make the mane. Add eyes and a felt nose. Use yarn to create a tail. Attach the head and tail to the body with small pieces of Velcro hook; the Velcro will let you interchange the lion's head and tail with the mouse's.

MOUSE PATTERN

MOUSE—Cut out the mouse's head and add a felt nose and whiskers. Twist a pipe cleaner around a pencil to make a curly tail. Attach small pieces of Velcro hook to the head and tail to interchange with the lion's head and tail.

POP-UP PUPPET

A puppet on a dowel stick can sing and dance to music, jump up and down, and even pop out and surprise you.

MATERIALS

Plastic or cardboard sewing cone (the type used on sergers) or large funnel, dowel (a size that suits your needs), spray paint or acrylic paint and brush, cotton print fabric, fabric glue, needle and thread, large pompon or Styrofoam ball, glue, scissors, trim or braiding, decorative materials (felt, plastic eyes, etc.)

DIRECTIONS

Spray paint the cone or brush on acrylic paint. Cut out fabric for your puppet and glue or sew together the sides with the wrong sides facing out. Leave the bottom open. Glue or sew on paws, hands, etc.

After the glue dries, turn the puppet body right-side out. Now dab glue on the end of the dowel and push the dowel into the puppet body. Squeeze the material around the end of the dowel. Dab glue on the bottom of the pompon or Styrofoam ball and press it over the end of the fabric-covered dowel.

Let the glue dry for several hours. When dry, add eyes, ears, mouth, etc., to the pompon to suit the character. Place the dowel through the large end of the painted cone and glue the bottom of the fabric to the cone. Cover the edge where fabric meets cone by gluing on trim or braiding. Decorate as desired.

STORY RETELLING

Put various pop-up puppets in the story corner and let the children tell their own stories. Their imaginations will soar as different pop-up characters are discovered in the center.

POP-UP PATTERN

CONE COVER

POP-UP PATTERN

SOCK PUPPET

Sock puppets are expressive and easy to make. They can also live in a variety of houses, such as coffee cans, boxes, and tubes.

MATERIALS

Old socks (tube socks works very well), glue, marker, decorative materials (plastic eyes, pieces of felt, etc.)

DIRECTIONS

Try to make this puppet out of a sock that fits your hand. Place your hand inside the sock, open your hand, and push the sock between your thumb and fingers. This space is the mouth. Mark spots to add eyes, hair, tongue, etc., to create the particular story character.

For two puppets in one— good to use with two characters who talk back and forth or for a character that metamorphoses—place one sock inside another and stitch or glue the cuffs together. Decorate as desired.

STORY RETELLING

The sock puppet can live in a playhouse made from a coffee can, a box, or a tube. Sock puppets are also particularly good for retelling stories about worms, snakes, or caterpillars like the story *The Very Hungry Caterpillar*. Place a sock puppet and its house in the story corner and listen to the children retell stories and create their own.

SOCK PUPPET IN A CAN

Permanently attaching a sock puppet to a coffee can home makes it durable as well as eye-catching. Just be sure can edges are smooth to the touch.

MATERIALS
Empty coffee can with both ends removed, heavy tape or duct tape, two plastic lids that fit the can, spray paint or acrylic paint and brush, glue, sock puppet, vinyl letters

DIRECTIONS
Clean the coffee can inside and out. Be sure the edges are smooth to the touch. If not, cover with heavy tape or duct tape. Be sure the plastic lids fit tight so you can store the puppet once the puppet has been put inside. Paint the can. When dry, glue your favorite sock puppet inside. Let the glue dry completely. Then glue on vinyl letters to give the puppet a name.

When the puppet is used for play, the can lids should be removed so the child can get a hand inside the sock. To store, press the puppet down inside the can and cover with the plastic lids.

STORY RETELLING
Let the children manipulate the puppet in its house. If the puppet is placed in the story center, the children will use it to help retell their favorite stories.

STICK PUPPET

Stick puppets are versatile—they can be short or tall, large or little, and pop out of houses or live on their own.

MATERIALS
Heavy paper or art foam
Glue
Laminator
Markers or paint
Scissors
Popsicle stick, tongue depressor or paint stirrer
Tape

DIRECTIONS
Draw and color a puppet shape on heavy paper and laminate. Or color a puppet pattern, laminate, and glue to a larger piece of art form. For a small puppet, glue the picture to a Popsicle stick; for a larger puppet, glue it to a tongue depressor or paint stirrer.

If you want to make puppet pictures interchangeable, tape a heavy piece of paper to the back of the art foam or laminated paper and leave the bottom open. Insert the stick into this tunnel for puppet use, and remove to use with a different puppet.

To use a stick puppet with a story board or magnetic board, remove the stick and add a small piece of Velcro hook or a self-adhesive magnet.

STORY RETELLING
Stick puppet characters can be housed in a can or a box and lend themselves to use with many stories.

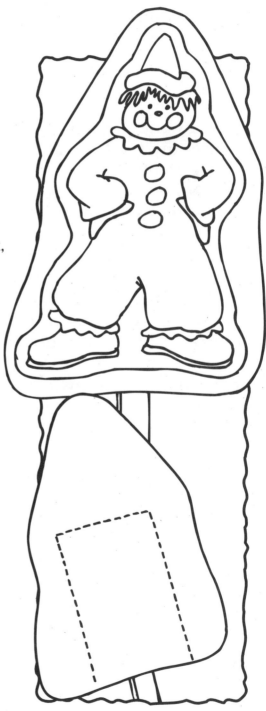

Storytelling © 1998 Monday Morning Books, Inc.

DOWN BY THE POND TALE

Sing to the tune of "Down by the Bay."

Down by the pond where the cattails grow,
Back to my boat I dare not go.
For if I do my grandpa will say,
"Did you ever see a fish
Eating from a dish, down by the pond?"

Down by the pond where the cattails grow,
Back to my boat I dare not go.
For if I do my grandpa will say,
"Did you ever see a snake
Licking a cake, down by the pond?"

Down by the pond where the cattails grow,
Back to my boat I dare not go.
For if I do my grandpa will say,
"Did you ever see a raccoon
Smiling at the moon, down by the pond?"

Down by the pond where the cattails grow,
Back to my boat I dare not go.
For if I do my grandpa will say,
"Did you ever see a frog
Kissing a dog, down by the pond?"

Down by the pond where the cattails grow,
Back to my boat I dare not go.
For if I do my grandpa will say,
"Did you ever try to rhyme
In the warm sunshine, down by the pond?"

STICK PUPPET PATTERNS

Copy patterns onto heavy paper, color, cut out, laminate, and glue sticks to the back. Use with the "Down by the Pond" tale.

Storytelling © 1998 Monday Morning Books, Inc.

STICK PUPPET PATTERNS

STICK PUPPET PATTERNS

STICK PUPPET PATTERNS

TUBE PUPPET

A variety of tubes and materials can be used to make these story puppets. Paper towel tubes and toilet tissue tubes are ideal for children to use as bases. When the puppets are ready to go home, you can attach a note that tells the parents about the story the child has chosen and the puppet he or she has made. Encourage family members to ask the child to retell the story using the puppet.

MATERIALS
Cardboard tubes
Markers
Paint and brushes
Scissors
Glue
Art foam
Wiggly eyes
Felt and pompons
Paper cupcake tin liners
A variety of decorative materials
Colored construction paper and tissue paper

DIRECTIONS
Let the children paint and then glue decorative materials to their cardboard tubes to represent favorite story characters. Tube puppets can represent people, animals, or fantasy figures.

STORY RETELLING
Provide the children with a favorite book and a special tube puppet character to retell the story with. Children may also want to use the puppets they make to put on a puppet show.

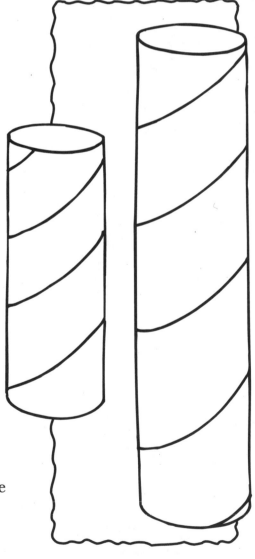

TUBE PUPPET EXAMPLES

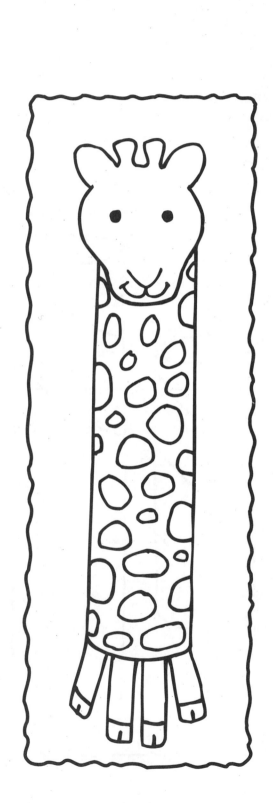

TUBE PUPPET EXAMPLES

Storytelling © 1998 Monday Morning Books, Inc.

COMMERCIAL PUPPETS

Commercial puppets are available through many educational stores, children's toy stores, discount stores, and catalogs. Purchasing a special puppet can enhance your storytelling corner. Child-size puppets are available and can enrich a child's story appreciation. But don't purchase a puppet just because it's cute. Only buy one if it will support your storytelling curriculum.

Commercial puppets range in size from tiny finger puppets to very large puppets. When you buy a puppet, always be sure that it fits your hand and is easy to manipulate. Work the puppet's mouth, check that the head turns, and see if it fits your hand and arm comfortably.

The following are a few of the types of commercial puppets available:

PEOPLE PUPPETS—Interchangeable people puppets are favorites because they are so easy to manipulate. One puppet can double as many others with just a change of outfits. People puppets come in different skin tones and with many changes of clothes.

PUPPETS THAT SWALLOW—Varmint (available from Playful Puppets) is a puppet that eats and swallows. He enjoys eating cookies and sometimes vegetables. He's a great mascot that children will enjoy having daily interaction and conversations with.

FUNZELS—Funzels are a unique type of silly puppet. They come in three different sizes and are kid-friendly. Funzels have large pop-eyes and wild hair. The middle-size puppet can be stored in a coffee can house. Baby Funzels can be housed in a finger puppet playhouse.

PART II

PROPS AND PLAYFUL TALES

STORYTELLING WITH PROPS

Props are an enhancement to any story corner and invite the children to get ready to hear and tell a good story. Props give children clues to what an upcoming story will focus on, and can also be used to start a conversation about a story, for example, "Looking at this honey jar, what do you think the story is about?" Props also help to develop language, listening, and speaking skills. Props aid in explaining images and words contained in stories.

Props also encourage children to participate in a story, both as a listener and as a speaker in retelling. As you choose stories to tell, look for those that encourage participation. Workable props can be found at almost any type of store: grocery, hardware, discount, crafts, teacher supply, and specialty stores, as well as hotel and museum gift shops. Many of the small items we use on a daily basis can also be recycled as props or used in prop creations children make for favorite stories. The props detailed in this section may motivate you to come up with additional ideas of your own.

If you and the children enjoy telling stories with a story board, prop cutouts can be made from felt, art foam, paper, magazine pictures, or hand-drawn images with a piece of Velcro attached to the back. Flannel-board characters and props that you have used in the past can be recycled by simply adding a Velcro square. Keeping a story board in the story corner will encourage children to manipulate the figures and think about stories in different ways.

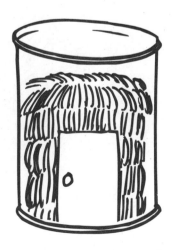  

STORY-STARTERS

Story-starters are special tools for signaling the beginning of storytelling time. A story-starter, such as a song or chant, a special prop, or a class mascot will invite the children to gather together.

One good story-starter to try is this simple chant:

STORY TIME CHANT

Hey, hey, what do you say?
Hey, hey, what do you say?
Hey, hey, what do you say?
I have a story for you today!

Hey, hey, what do you say?
Hey, hey, what do you say?
Hey, hey, what do you say?
Now it's time for story play.

STORY-STARTER PUPPETS

Below and on the following pages are some examples of character story-starters that can be made from inexpensive and easily purchased materials. Use these examples as a springboard for your own creativity.

LARRY LION—This mop-head replacement can be purchased at any local discount store. It has two holes on the back where your fingers can be inserted for easy manipulation. The eyes are made with large pompons, the nose from a medium-size pompon, and the mouth from a piece of art foam.

STORY-STARTER PUPPETS

MADAME BELINDA AND MADAME MELINDA—These items (a plastic bottle and window wiper) can be purchased at grocery, hardware, and discount stores. Add two eyes, a nose, and a mouth cut from art foam, some curly yarn hair, and a small hat purchased at a crafts store. Using a high-pitched voice with these story-starters is very effective.

BETTY BUTTERFLY—This butterfly story-starter is made with one shoulder pad and two heel pads, which can be purchased at most drugstores or discount stores.

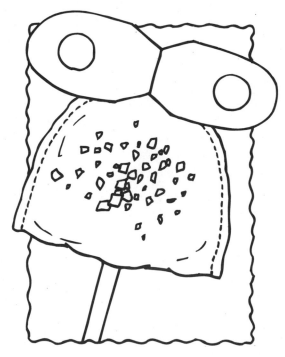

STORY-STARTER PUPPETS

MOP PEOPLE—Mop people are excellent motivators for storytelling participation. The mop person on the left is Peter Pirate; the one on the right is Ms. Maryland Mop. Small mops can be found at discount stores.

FANCY FANNY—This cute story-starter is made from a dowel, a Styrofoam ball, a small mop-head replacement, a straw hat, and earrings, all of which can be purchased at a crafts store or discount store. The face is drawn on with a permanent marker.

STORY-STARTER PUPPETS

DISHPAN DAN—Dishpan Dan is made out of a small kitchen mop that is used to clean dishes. Wiggly eyes and some curly yarn hair have been glued on, and a nose and mouth added with paint.

MOLLY MOP—Molly is a mop-head replacement with pompon eyes and nose and a mouth made from a piece of red, glued-on art foam. Pony beads have been strung throughout Molly's hair, a project the children can undertake. Children may wish to continue to experiment with this story-starter's hair decorations.

STORY-STARTER PUPPETS

DANDY DUSTERS—The characters shown here are just a few of the low-cost duster story-starters you can create. Use your imagination to add eyes, nose, mouth, hair, hat, and clothes.

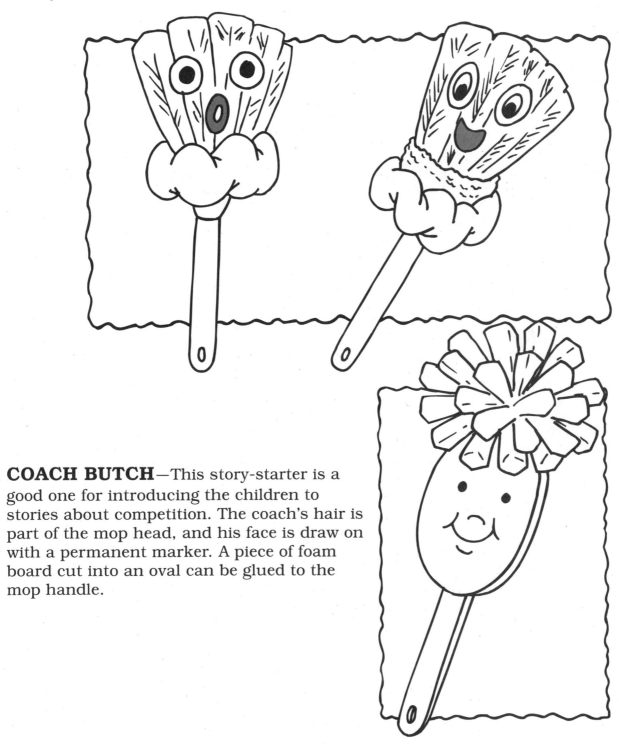

COACH BUTCH—This story-starter is a good one for introducing the children to stories about competition. The coach's hair is part of the mop head, and his face is draw on with a permanent marker. A piece of foam board cut into an oval can be glued to the mop handle.

STORY-STARTER PUPPETS

FLUFF AND PUFF—Fluff and Puff are made from kitchen mops. Puff has two Ping-Pong balls for eyes on which black centers have been drawn with a permanent marker. Fluff's eyes are made from two medium-sized pompons and the nose and mouth are drawn on a cap. A soft, slow voice is effective for use with Puff and a high-pitched, whiny voice with Fluff.

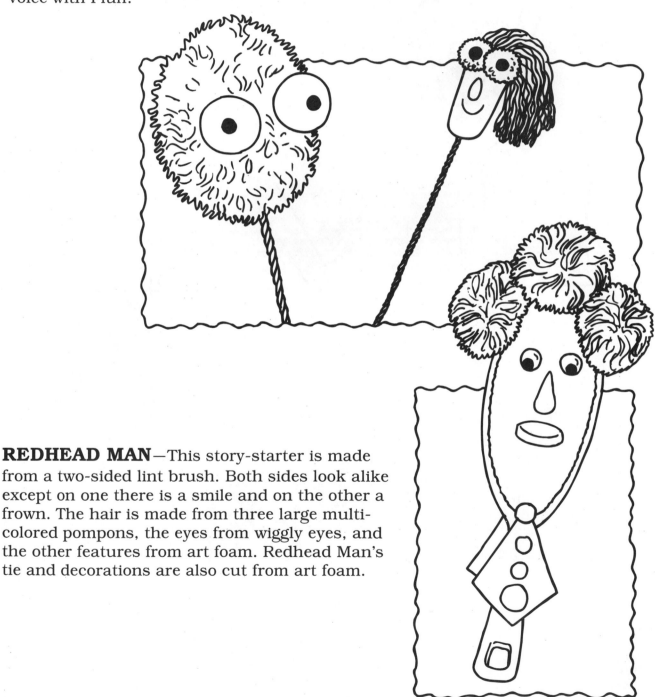

REDHEAD MAN—This story-starter is made from a two-sided lint brush. Both sides look alike except on one there is a smile and on the other a frown. The hair is made from three large multi-colored pompons, the eyes from wiggly eyes, and the other features from art foam. Redhead Man's tie and decorations are also cut from art foam.

CATERPILLAR-TO-BUTTERFLY PROPS

When metamorphosis is part of the story, these props help in the telling and retelling.

MATERIALS

1 green paint roller, 3 green pipe cleaners, 1 black pipe cleaner, 2 white Ping-Pong balls, 2 wiggly eyes, glue, scissors, toilet paper roll, green construction paper, several shades of green tissue paper, green tape, black felt, white coffee filter, non-pinch-style clothespin, markers, squirt bottle, water

DIRECTIONS

Caterpillar—Space out the three green pipe cleaners and glue them around the paint roller to make the roller look like it's segmented. Glue the two Ping-Pong balls and the wiggly eyes to the front of the body. Bend the black pipe cleaner in half and add for antenna. The version #2 butterfly can be rolled up and stored inside the caterpillar.

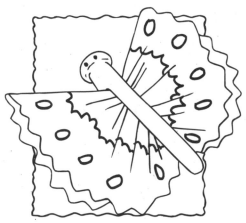

Butterfly #1—Cover the toilet paper roll with green construction paper. Cut out and glue on black felt eyes and glue on layers of green tissue paper for wings.

Butterfly #2—Use markers to add colors or designs to the coffee filter. Squirt with water and let dry. Crumple the filter slightly and insert into the clothespin. Fluff out the tissue paper wings. Add color or drawings to the clothespin body if desired. The completed butterfly can be stored inside the paint-roller caterpillar to emerge at the appropriate time.

STORY RETELLING

Children can create individual caterpillar and butterfly props to take home to share with their families. Attach a note to the props encouraging parents to listen to their child's story and to read a suggested story together. In the story corner, provide caterpillar and butterfly props and a copy of *The Very Hungry Caterpillar*.

PATTERNS

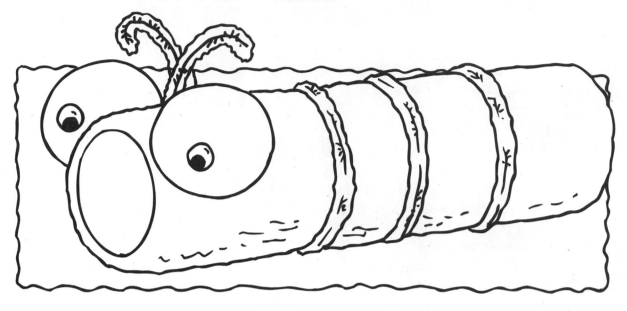

CATERPILLAR

BUTTERFLY

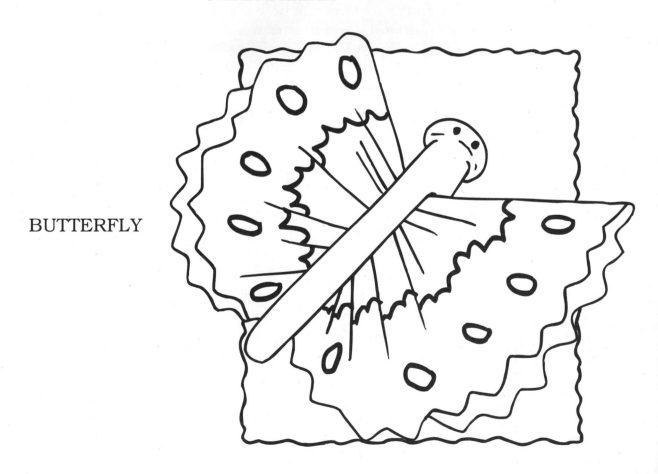

COFFEE CAN HOUSES AND TALE

BASIC CONSTRUCTION

A coffee can makes a durable puppet house. Use coffee cans to store puppets and props in the story corner.

MATERIALS
Empty coffee can with plastic lid
Heavy tape or duct tape
Paint primer
Spray paint
Permanent markers or acrylic paint and brushes
Clear sealer

DIRECTIONS
Clean the coffee can. Cover rough edges with heavy tape or duct tape. Paint the can with primer and let dry. Then paint the can the desired color.

If you're making a house for a particular puppet or story, add art work to fit the story. When dry, label the can, spray it with a clear sealer, and fill with puppets or props. Cover with the plastic lid.

STORY RETELLING
Place coffee can houses in the story corner and rotate them.

THREE PIGS' HOUSES

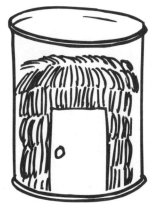

Storytelling © 1998 Monday Morning Books, Inc.

NURSERY RHYME PROP CANS

HOLIDAY PROP CANS

THEME PROP CANS

SEA LIFE

OUTER SPACE

LOG

HONEY JAR

HONEY JAR TALE AND PROPS

Have the children make art foam puppets from the patterns on the following pages. Puppets with magnets can be manipulated on the Honey Jar coffee can (p. 60).

WHO TOOK THE HONEY FROM THE HONEY JAR?

"Who took the honey from the honey jar?"

"POSSUM took the honey from the honey jar."
"Who me?"
"Yeah, you!"
"Not me!"
"Then who?"

"RACCOON took the honey from the honey jar."
"Who me?"
"Yeah, you!"
"Not me!"
"Then who?"

"RABBIT took the honey from the honey jar."
"Who me?"
"Yeah, you!"
"Not me!"
"Then who?"

"SQUIRREL took the honey from the honey jar."
"Who me?"
"Yeah, you!"
"Not me!"
"Then who?"

"BEAR took the honey from the honey jar."
"Who me?"
"Yeah, you!"
"Yeah, me!"
"I took the honey from the honey jar."
"Yum! Yum! Yum!"

PATTERNS

POSSUM

RACCOON

PATTERNS

SQUIRREL

RABBIT

PATTERN

BEAR

SMALL CAN HOUSES AND PUPPETS

Children can create their own storytelling houses and characters using a variety of small cans. An adult may need to paint on a base coat before the children begin.

MATERIALS
Assorted small cans with plastic lids
Heavy tape or duct tape
Paint primer
Spray paint or acrylic paint and brushes
Clear sealer
Art items (art foam, wiggly eyes, yarn, felt, buttons, feathers)

DIRECTIONS
Clean the can inside and out and remove the label. Brush on primer. Then paint the can the desired color. If the can will be used as a puppet, add features like those of a favorite story character. If acrylic paint is used, coat when dry with a clear sealer. Use art foam for adding arms and legs.

STORY RETELLING
Mix these small can houses and puppets with coffee can houses in the story corner to create interest. The props and puppets will aid in a wide variety of story retelling.

EXAMPLES

SOUP CAN BUNNY

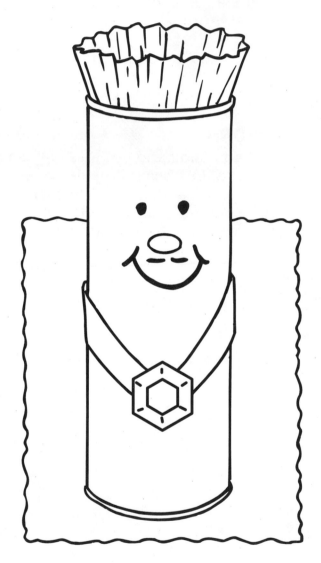

SMALL CAN FROG

CHIP CAN KING

CIRCLE TIME PROPS

When it's circle time, these props can help children take turns creating a story.

MATERIALS
Coffee can
Spray paint
Wooden spoons (one for each child)
Nontoxic clear spray sealer
Permanent markers

DIRECTIONS
Spray paint the coffee can. Spray the spoons with clear sealer. Then let the children draw a picture of their face on the back of a spoon and print their name on the inside bowl. Place all the spoons in the coffee can and keep in the story corner.

STORYTELLING
Encourage the children to find their spoons and gather for circle time. Remind the children to keep their spoons in their laps while others are speaking. Begin the story by saying, "Once upon a time. . . "

Pass the story from one spoon storyteller to another. Children can hold up their spoons when they are telling the story. Be sure that each child gets a chance to add to the story.

Collect the spoons and return them to the can.

STORY RETELLING
The children can take their spoons home over a holiday break. When they return to class, let each child take a turn telling about his or her holiday adventures. The spoons can also be used at home for child-parent storytelling. Send a note home with each spoon to encourage the sharing of a special story.

COPY PAPER BOX HOUSE

Copy paper boxes make excellent puppet houses. They're roomy and sturdy and their lids can become roofs.

MATERIALS

Empty copy paper box
Spray paint or acrylic paint and brushes
Permanent markers

DIRECTIONS

Paint the box a suitable color for a house in a favorite story. The lid can be painted a contrasting color. Use permanent markers to add features such as windows, doors, window boxes, front door lights, and roof tiles.

STORY RETELLING

When kept in the story corner, paper-box houses can be used for story retelling. Houses can also store a variety of small puppets and props.

PILLOWCASE HOUSE

For a puppet house that's soft to the touch as well as easy to move around, a pillowcase does the trick.

MATERIALS
Pillowcase, sponges, paint

DIRECTIONS
Let the children take turns sponge-painting the pillowcase to resemble a house from a favorite story. Let dry thoroughly before putting it to use.

STORY RETELLING
This soft, flexible house can be moved to different locations as the children retell a story. Puppets and story props can be stored inside.

Children sponge-painting pillowcase.

EXAMPLES

SUN

FARM

OCEAN

SPACE

DINOSAURS

SHOE BOX HOUSE

A shoe box can be transformed into a puppet house that's just the right size for small hands to put figures into. Shoe boxes can also be turned into puppets or story props.

MATERIALS
Large shoe box
Sponges and paint or acrylic paint and brushes
Permanent markers
Glue
Scissors
Art items (yarn, art foam, felt, wiggly eyes, and cotton balls)

DIRECTIONS
Paint the box an appropriate color for the story; sponge-painting works very well on this surface. If the box will be used as a house, add features with markers or pens. Windows and doors can be cut out or partially cut to open. If the box will be used as a puppet or prop, glue on necessary materials.

STORY RETELLING
Set the box and its storybook in the story corner. Encourage the children to use it as they retell the story. Puppets and props can be stored inside.

AESOP'S FABLE BOX

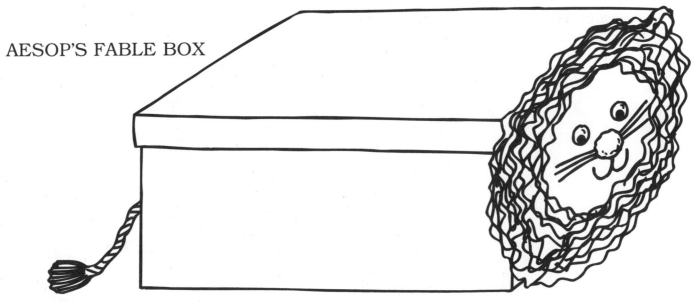

PLAYFUL FROG HOUSE, TALE, AND PROPS

MATERIALS
Coffee can
Spray paint
Acrylic paint and brushes
Permanent marker

DIRECTIONS
Paint the can to look like a pond scene, with a frog sitting on a log. Label the can with the title of its tale. The story props can be housed in the can.

STORY RETELLING
Encourage the children to use the puppets and props with the pond scene to retell the story. The story can also be retold using commercially made props. Plastic or rubber caterpillars, fish, and frogs can be purchased at most school-supply or nature stores. If the mosquitoes make a loud buzzing sound when the story is originally told. The children will want to retell it many times. Once you have taught the children the repeated verse, they will want to come up with their own versions.

PLAYFUL FROG TALE

by Mary Jo Huff

Once upon a day, a little frog was sitting quietly on a big old log. It was time for lunch and the frog was really hungry. He noticed a small lizard sunning himself on the end of the log. He hopped over to the lizard and said:

I'm a hungry little frog.
And you're bothering my log.
I don't want to fight,
But if you don't watch out,
I'll just take a bite.

The hungry frog flicked out his quick tongue and gobbled up that little lizard.

But the frog was STILL hungry. He looked around and saw a fuzzy caterpillar crawling up the side of the log. He hopped over to the caterpillar and said:

I'm a hungry little frog.
And you're bothering my log.
I don't want to fight,
But if you don't watch out,
I'll just take a bite.

With a quick flick of his tongue, the hungry frog gobbled up that fuzzy caterpillar.

But the frog was STILL hungry. He spotted a dragonfly resting on the end of the log. He hopped over to the dragonfly and said:

I'm a hungry little frog.
And you're bothering my log.
I don't want to fight,
But if you don't watch out,
I'll just take a bite.

The frog's tongue was quicker than the wings of the dragonfly, and the frog gobbled the dragonfly up.

But the little frog was STILL hungry. He heard a swarm of mosquitoes hovering close to the top of the log. He quietly hopped near the swarm and said:

I'm a hungry little frog.
And you're bothering my log.
I don't want to fight,
But if you don't watch out,
I'll just take a bite.

Before the swarm could move, the frog swallowed every one of the mosquitoes with one quick flick of his tongue.

But the little frog was STILL hungry. A small fish swam close to the log. The little frog hopped up to the fish and said:

I'm a hungry little frog.
And you're bothering my log.
I don't want to fight,
But if you don't watch out,
I'll just take a bite.

That little fish laughed and dared the frog to take a bite. The frog leaped toward the little fish but the fish swam away and hid behind some rocks. The little frog swam after the fish but could not find him. As the frog searched for the little fish, along came a BIG FISH, who looked at the little frog and said:

I'm a BIG OLE FISH
With a hungry wish.
I don't want to fight,
But if you don't watch out,
I'll just take a bite.

The frightened little frog swam to the top of the water and leaped upon his log. He was grateful to be a quiet little frog, just sitting on his log.

PATTERNS

The following patterns can be used to create puppets and props out of art foam. Adding Velcro hook to each completed pattern will make it suitable for use with a story board or story apron. Adding a magnet to each piece will enable it to be used on the can or on a magnetic board.

LOG

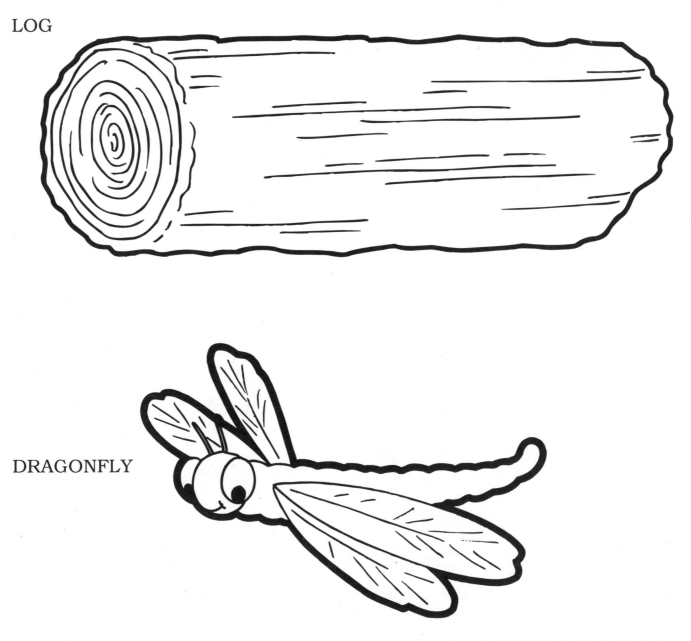

DRAGONFLY

PATTERNS

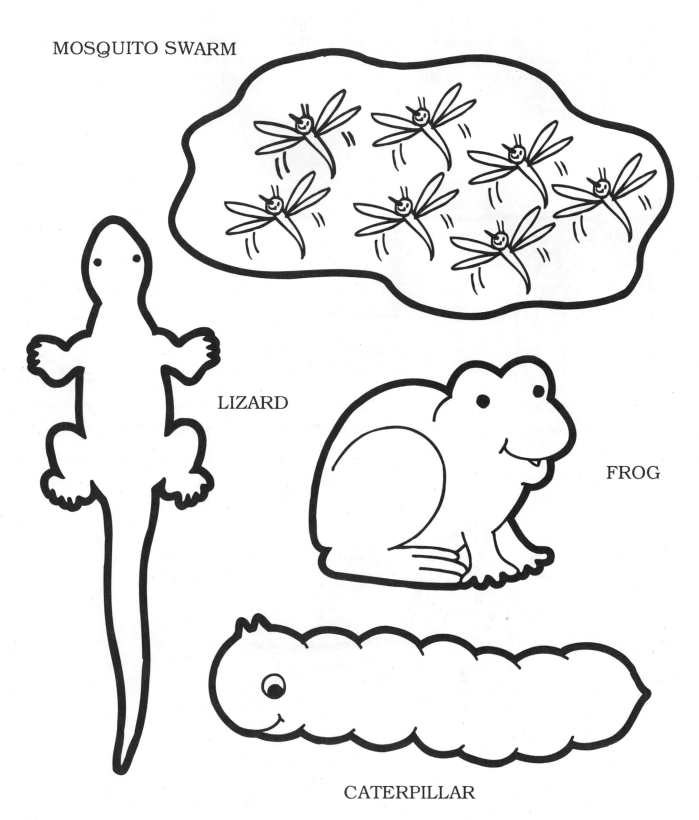

MOSQUITO SWARM

LIZARD

FROG

CATERPILLAR

PATTERNS

FISH

BIG FISH

JOHNNY CAKE MAN PROPS AND TALE

This imaginative story will be hard for children to resist.

MATERIALS
2 sturdy white paper plates
6 metal spatulas
Art foam
Stapler
Scissors
Self-adhesive magnets
Brown paint (watercolor, tempera, or acrylic)
Brush
Markers

DIRECTIONS
Cut characters from art foam, and outline features with permanent marker. Add a magnet square to the back of each character. Paint the paper plates brown. When dry, cut one in half. Staple one half to the full plate to form a pocket for storing the characters. Glue the Johnny Cake pattern to the front of the paper plate.

STORY RETELLING
Store the Johnny Cake, puppets, and spatulas in the story corner. As the children retell this tale, have them place each character on a spatula as it enters the story. The magnets will keep the puppets on the spatulas. As the children participate in the story retelling, record their versions on cassettes.

PATTERN

JOHNNY CAKE MAN

PATTERNS

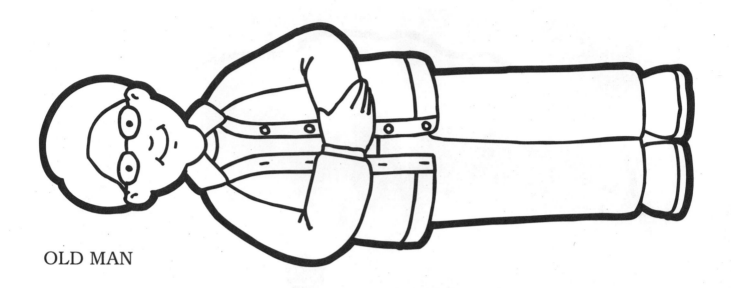

OLD MAN

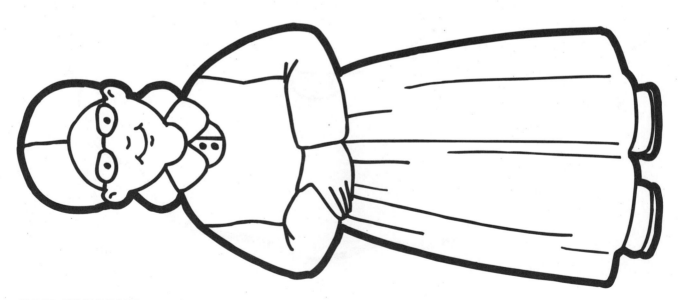

OLD WOMAN

PATTERNS

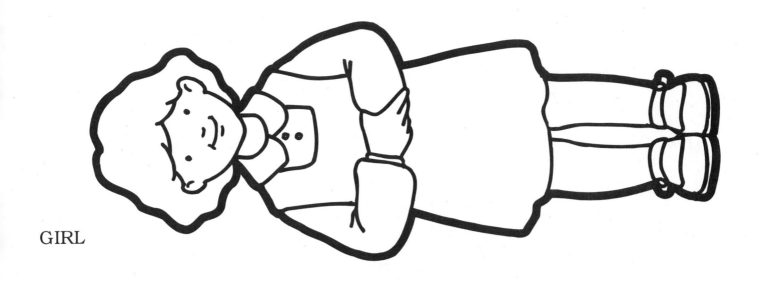

GIRL

COW

PATTERNS

HORSE

FOX

PIG

JOHNNY CAKE TALE
adapted by Mary Jo Huff

There once was an old woman, an old man, and their daughter. They all lived on a farm near a big river. One morning, the old woman decided to make a Johnny Cake for the family. She wanted to teach her daughter the recipe.

"Oh, boy!" exclaimed the little girl. "This Johnny Cake will taste delicious!"

The young girl and the old woman rolled the dough thin, cut out a Johnny Cake, and put it in the oven to bake. The old woman warned her daughter not to open the oven door until the Johnny Cake was done baking.

The old woman went outside to help the old man feed the animals. The little girl smelled the Johnny Cake and decided to take just a little peek. She opened the oven door just a tiny bit, and the Johnny Cake rolled out. "Stop! Stop! Come back!" yelled the little girl.

The Johnny Cake rolled out the door, across the porch, and down the barnyard path. The old woman, the old man, and their daughter ran after the Johnny Cake as fast as they could run.

"RUN, RUN, AS FAST AS YOU CAN, YOU CAN'T CATCH ME, I'M THE JOHNNY CAKE MAN."

Soon the Johnny Cake Man came upon a PIG.
"Why are you running away?" asked the pig.

"I've run away from the old woman, the old man, and their daughter, and I can run away from you," said the Johnny Cake Man.

"You think so?" said the pig. And the pig began to chase the Johnny Cake Man.

"RUN, RUN, AS FAST AS YOU CAN, YOU CAN'T CATCH ME, I'M THE JOHNNY CAKE MAN."

The old woman, the old man, the young daughter, and the pig all ran fast, but they could not catch him. Soon the Johnny Cake Man came upon a COW in the pasture.

"Why are you running away?" asked the cow.
"I ran away from the old woman, the old man, the daughter, and the pig, and I can run away from you," said the Johnny Cake Man.

"Oh, you think so!" said the cow.

"RUN, RUN, AS FAST AS YOU CAN, YOU CAN'T CATCH ME, I'M THE JOHNNY CAKE MAN."

The cow ran fast, but she could not catch the Johnny Cake Man. The Johnny Cake Man ran past a HORSE galloping in the field. "Why are you running away?" asked the horse.

"I've run away from the old woman, the old man, the daughter, the pig, and the cow, and now I am going to run away from you," said the Johnny Cake Man.

"Oh, you think so!" said the horse, and he began to chase the Johnny Cake Man.

"RUN, RUN, AS FAST AS YOU CAN, YOU CAN'T CATCH ME, I'M THE JOHNNY CAKE MAN."

The horse ran fast, but he could not catch the Johnny Cake Man. Soon the Johnny Cake Man met a fox getting a drink at the river.

"Why are you running away?" asked the fox.

"I've run away from the old woman, the old man, the daughter, the pig, the cow, and the horse, and now I will run away from you," said the Johnny Cake Man.

"How will you cross the river?" asked the sly fox.
"I don't know," said the Johnny Cake Man.

"Hop on my back and I will take you across the river," the fox told him.

The Johnny Cake Man rolled up onto the fox's back and they began to cross the river. As the river deepened, the Johnny Cake Man rolled up the fox's back until he was on top of the fox's head. The sly fox raised his head and the Johnny Cake Man rolled down his nose and right into the fox's mouth.

The Johnny Cake Man ran away from the old woman, the old man, the daughter, the pig, the cow, and the horse, but he did not run away from the sly old fox.

Since all Johnny Cakes are made to be eaten, the fox had the best snack of all.

MOUSE HOUSE PROPS AND TALE

Glove puppets and a small can house add to the fun of the telling of this very interactive tale.

MATERIALS
Small can, paint, brush, 1 gray glove and 1 white or black glove, wiggly eyes (tiny and big), fishing line, gray felt, art foam, glue, scissors

DIRECTIONS
House—Paint the small can and cut out a mouse hole.

Mice—Use the gray glove for the five mice. Add wiggly eyes and a yarn tail to each mouse. Add felt noses and fishing line whiskers.

Cat—Use a white or black glove that fits your hand. The fingers will point down and be the cat's paws. The thumb will be the tail. On the body of the glove, glue on eyes, an art foam nose and ears, and fishing line whiskers.

When the cat enters the story, twirl the thumb tail as it approaches the mice. Hold up all five fingers to show how many mice live in the hole. Hold up one finger when the mouse shouts, "Scat!" Wiggle all five fingers when the mice scurry back to their house.

STORY RETELLING
Keep the mouse house and the glove puppets in the story corner for acting out this cat and mouse story.

MOUSE HOUSE TALE
by Mary Jo Huff

Five little mice were hiding in a hole
Waiting to nibble from a dinner bowl.

When it was dark and every light was out
One little mouse could be heard to shout:

"Dinner is served, let's all scurry!"
The cat might come, so the mice had to hurry.

A lookout was chosen to spot the cat.
The others all ate, until they heard, "SCAT, SCAT!"

The warning was loud, announcing cat trouble,
And five little mice disappeared on the double.

Those furry fat mice gathered back in their hole,
Bellies all full from the dinner bowl.

They patiently waited for the cat to go away,
Then the five little mice came out to play.

FARMER'S HEADACHE PIZZA BOX PROPS AND TALE

The children will love to make the animal sounds that bring this farmyard story to life. The story can be told using a pizza box lid as a story board or with a storytelling apron. The pizza box may be used for many other types of stories.

MATERIALS

Medium or large pizza box
Paint (spray paint works best)
Fabric glue
Velcro fabric and hook
Markers
Scissors
Art foam

DIRECTIONS

Spray paint the pizza box. Cut a square of Velcro fabric to fit inside the box lid and glue it on. Let the glue dry completely. Copy the patterns, lay them on top of the art foam, and cut them out. Outline the characters. Attach a small piece of Velcro hook to the back of each character. Store all the characters in the pizza box and use the inside lid for telling the story. Label the box with pictures so the children who cannot read can recognize the story.

STORY RETELLING

Provide the children with the pizza box and the story characters. Two children can retell the story by attaching each character to the box's inside lid as it enters the tale.

FARMER'S HEADACHE TALE
by Mary Jo Huff

There was a farmer who had a headache because his children were so noisy. He decided to go to his doctor and get a remedy for his throbbing headache.

The doctor told the farmer to get himself a horse and to bring the horse into the house. The farmer went out to the pasture and found a horse and brought the horse back to the house. But the noise from the horse (NEIGHHH!) was too loud.

The farmer returned to the doctor for a new remedy. This time the doctor said to get a cow. The farmer went home and brought a cow into the house. The noise from the cow (MOOOO!) was more than he could bear.

"THE HORSE WENT NEIGHHH!" (children)
"THE COW WENT MOOOOO!" (children)

The farmer returned to the doctor for a new remedy. This time the doctor told the farmer to get a pig. The farmer brought a pig into the house, but the noise the pig made was unbearable. That pig went OINNNNNK! all day long.

"THE HORSE WENT NEIGHHH!" (children)
"THE COW WENT MOOOOO!" (children)
"THE PIG WENT OINNNNNK!" (children)

The farmer went back to the doctor for a better remedy. The doctor said to bring a dog into the house. The farmer followed the doctor's orders and brought the dog into the house. The dog barked all day and evening (RUFFFFF!).

"THE HORSE WENT NEIGHHH!" (children)
"THE COW WENT MOOOOO!" (children)
"THE PIG WENT OINNNNNK!" (children)
"THE DOG WENT RUFFFFF!" (children)

This went on all day and all night. The farmer could not get any peace and quiet. He returned to the doctor for a new remedy and the doctor told him to get a cat. So, the farmer brought the cat into the house. That cat screeched MEOOWWW! and the dog chased her around and around the house.

"THE HORSE WENT NEIGHHH!" (children)
"THE COW WENT MOOOOO!" (children)
"THE PIG WENT OINNNNNK!" (children)
"THE DOG WENT RUFFFFF!" (children)
"THE CAT WENT MEOOWWW!" (children)

The farmer decided to ask the doctor just one more time. The doctor shrugged and suggested the farmer get a quiet mouse. So the farmer brought a tiny little mouse into the house. The cat heard the mouse squeeeeking and said, "MEOOWWW!" (children), the dog heard the cat and began to "RUFFFFF" (children), the pig heard the dog and began to "OINNNNNK!" (children), the cow heard the pig and began to "MOOOOO!" (children), and the horse heard the commotion and began to "NEIGHHH!" (children).

All the noise was too much for the farmer, so he put all the animals into the barnyard and enjoyed the quiet of his farmhouse. All he could hear were the sweet voices of his children and wife. The animals stayed in the barnyard and the farmer never had a headache again.

PATTERNS

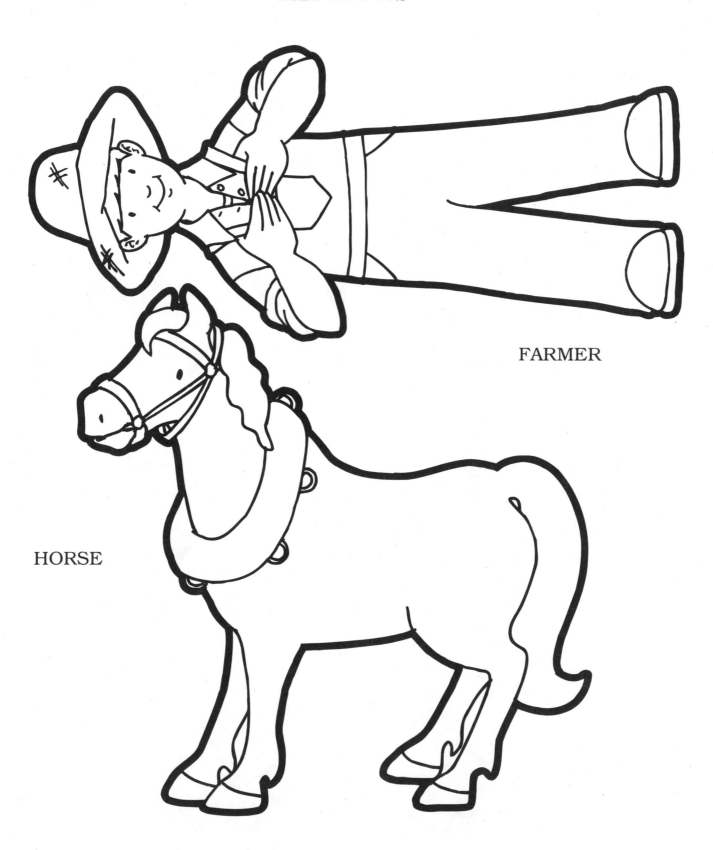

FARMER

HORSE

PATTERNS

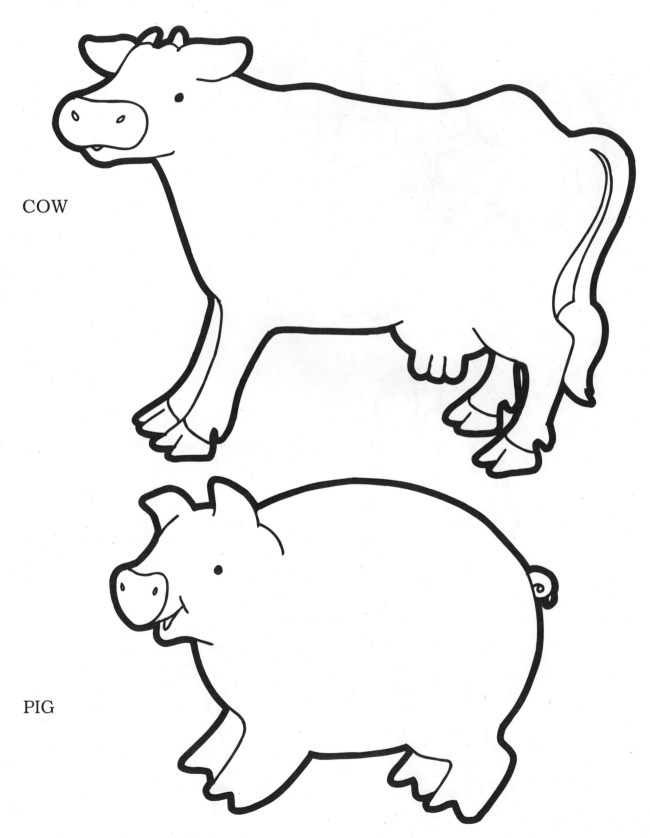

COW

PIG

PATTERNS

DOG

CAT

MOUSE

FIVE LITTLE SPECKLED FROGS
PROPS AND TALE

The story of the little speckled frogs will invite children to jump right in and participate.

MATERIALS
Empty coffee can
Brown spray paint
Black paint and brush
Green art foam
Self-adhesive magnets
Scissors
Marker

DIRECTIONS
Paint the coffee can brown. When dry, spatter it with black paint to resemble a log. Cut out five frogs from the art foam and add a magnet to the back of each. Use a marker to add specks to the frogs. When you tell the story, begin with all five frogs on the log and take one off at a time.

STORY RETELLING
Provide the children with the coffee can log with the art foam frogs stored inside. Let them invent their own ways to retell this simple story.

PATTERNS

FIVE LITTLE SPECKLED FROGS TALE
adapted by Mary Jo Huff

Five little speckled frogs,
Sitting on a hollow log,
Eating a most delicious meal.

One jumped into the creek,
The other frogs all said EEEK!
Now there were … (pause)
Just four speckled frogs.

Four little speckled frogs,
Sitting on a hollow log,
Eating a most delicious meal.

One jumped into the creek,
The other frogs all said EEEK!
Now there were …
Just three speckled frogs.

Three little speckled frogs,
Sitting on a hollow log,
Eating a most delicious meal.

One jumped into the creek,
The other frogs all said EEEK!
Now there were …
Just two speckled frogs.

Two little speckled frogs,
Sitting on a hollow log,
Eating a most delicious meal.

One jumped into the creek,
The other frog didn't speak.
He was just a …
Lonely little speckled frog.

PART III

STORY CORNERS
AND PLAYFUL TALES

CREATING A STORY CORNER

The story corner provides the storytellers and the children with a special place to enter the world of language, imagination, and creative drama. Create your story corner to fit your needs. Adapt the following ideas to suit you, your children, and the space and resources you have available. Children develop language and art skills, interact with the teacher and each other, and have fun using their imaginations.

SEATING—The storyteller can stand or sit on a chair, stool, or rocker. The listeners may sit on a special story rug, the floor, a quilt, or a story sheet.

EQUIPMENT—A well-equipped story corner should contain:
- storytelling apron
- storytelling mitt
- puppet mascot
- puppet stage
- story board
- magnetic board
- tape recorder
- musical instruments

STORY-STARTERS—Story-starters help children get ready for story time.

PROPS—Props should always be available for the storyteller. Some props may announce an upcoming story. Props will increase interest in, and encourage participation in, the story.

PUPPETS—Puppets make stories come alive, and are one of the most powerful tools for the storyteller. Puppets should have a special place in the story corner.

ORGANIZING—Include a story file in the story corner. This file should contain information for future reference.

STORY RUG—Children can sit on their own special story rug—a carpet remnant. Names can be added with fabric paint.

STORY CLUES—Story clues posted around the room can create interest for an upcoming story. Small pictures to which you add a piece of Velcro hook can be placed on a Velcro story board or taped to poster board.

STORY BOXES—Children delight in decorating shoe, cereal, or other boxes with scenes from their favorite stories. Boxes can be kept in the story center for story retelling.

BUILDING A STORY WALL

A portable story wall may be just what you need. By standing it at an angle from the wall, you create a storytelling area that you can set up at story time. Place area rugs or carpet remnants in the space. The wall can be moved, and can be reversed.

CONSTRUCTION MATERIALS FOR A PORTABLE WALL

4' x 6' sheet of pegboard
4' x 6' sheet of plywood
2" x 6" x 8' board—for base
2" x 6" x 8' board—for top
2" x 4" x 6' board—for sides and center
2" x 4" x 6' board—for bottom braces
3 heavy-duty locking casters
molding strip—to cover seam in center
Velcro fabric
corkboard or ceiling tiles
box or wood for flower box (optional)
cardboard or fabric for window dressing
multi-pocket shoe holder

Metric Measurements for Portable Wall:
1.5 meter x 2 meter sheet of pegboard
1.5 meter x 2 meter sheet of plywood
150 x 50 ml x 2.5 meter board - for base
150 x 50 ml x 2.5 m board - for top
100 x 50 ml x 2 m board - for sides and center
100 x 50 ml x 2 m board - for bottom braces

PORTABLE WALL SECTIONS

Side 1:

Corkboard section. The upper left corner of the wall can be used as an announcement board. Information of any kind can be pinned there: when story time will be, who the storyteller will be, any daily information, photos of the children, drawings, and so on.

Velcro section. This lower area should be covered with Velcro fabric. A seated storyteller can use it as a story board, Velcro puppets or props can be displayed there, announcements or art projects can be featured—it can be used in a variety of ways. Children can manipulate story characters at this level.

Puppet window. The upper right corner of the wall will contain the puppet window opening. The puppeteer will stand on the other side of the opening and show the puppets through it.

Puppet storage. The lower right corner holds the puppets. A multi-pocket shoe holder will provide a home for a number of puppets.

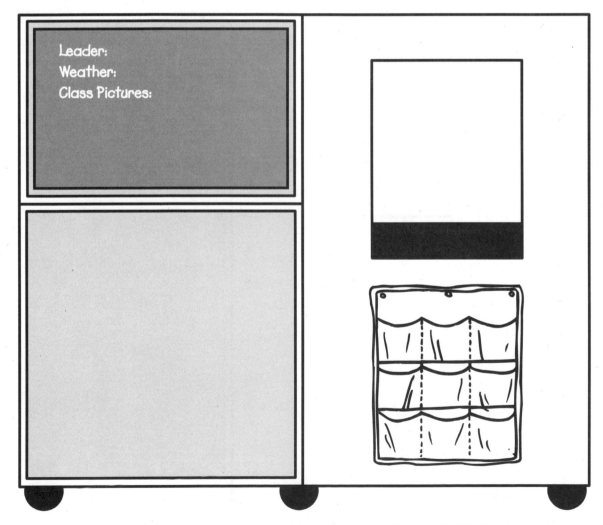

Leader:

Weather:

Class Pictures:

PORTABLE WALL SECTIONS

Side 2:

Pegboard section. Pegboard is used in the upper right corner of the wall. The area can hold hooks for props or other materials.

Velcro section. The lower right corner should be covered with Velcro fabric. The storyteller can sit on the floor and use the Velcro area for storytelling.

Puppet window. Make the window cutout on the upper left side large enough for several puppets to be seen through it but still conceal the puppeteer. Shutters or fabric curtains are a nice added feature.

Under-window area. A small window box can be attached at the base of the window opening to display paper flowers, store props, or story clues. The area below can be covered with cork or ceiling tiles to display pinned-up items.

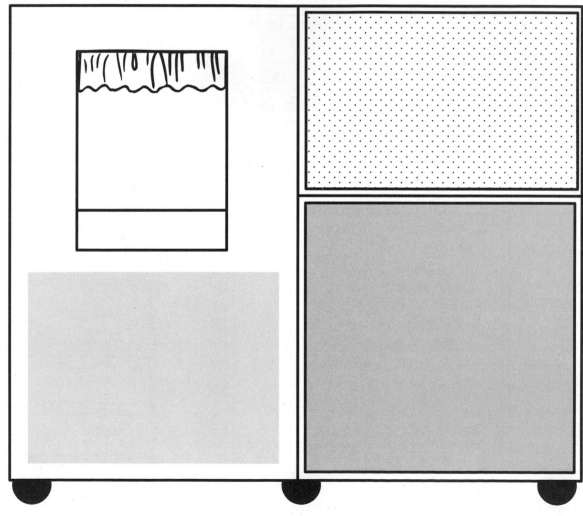

SETTING UP A STORY FILE

A story file will not only keep track of all the stories you have developed for storytelling; it will also remind you of the particular puppets and props that have been created and can be used with them.

To set up a story file, use a suitable box and filing cards. The following example shows the type of information you may want to include about each story in your repertoire.

TITLE _____

AUTHOR _____

PUBLISHER_____ DATE_____

PROPS_____

PUPPETS _____

COMMENTS_____

STORYTELLING APRON AND TALE

Storytelling can be very exciting with the interactive storytelling apron. The storyteller actually wears the story board, and story puppets and props appear from inside the pockets.

MATERIALS

Apron pattern
1 yard (.9 m) Velcro fabric
1/2 yard (.5 m) cotton twill
2 1/2 yards (2.3 m) soft cloth string
Safety pin
Spool of thread
Scissors
Sewing machine

DIRECTIONS

Cut out the apron pieces according to the pattern. Sew together using a zigzag stitch with the soft, or loop, side of the Velcro facing out. Hem the bottom edge of the cotton twill and turn up to create the pockets (the depth of the pockets can be adjusted by cutting out a larger or smaller piece of cotton twill). Make two seams to create three pockets and overstitch to reinforce. Turn the curved areas of the apron under one inch (2.5 cm) and stitch down to create tunnels. Turn the straight edges under and stitch down. Thread the soft cloth string through the tunnels using a large safety pin at one end to pull it through. The string allows you to adjust the apron to fit. Puppets and props that are placed on the apron must have a piece of Velcro with the rough, or hook, side facing out.

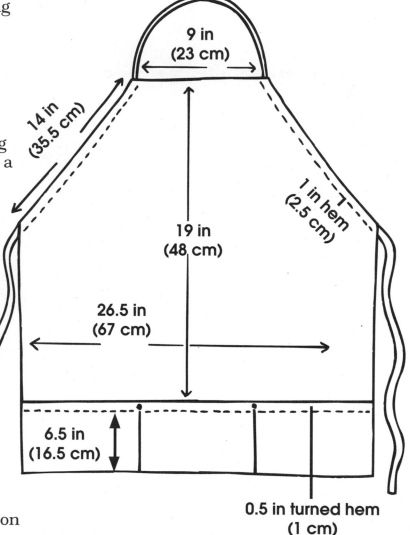

9 in (23 cm)

14 in (35.5 cm)

1 in hem (2.5 cm)

19 in (48 cm)

26.5 in (67 cm)

6.5 in (16.5 cm)

0.5 in turned hem (1 cm)

USING THE APRON

Storytelling with the apron provides children with creative, hands-on literature experiences.

PREPARATIONS
• Choose a story with 8 to 10 main characters and props. Having too many pieces on the apron can distract both the teller and the listeners.
• Create story puppets and props from laminated paper, poster board, felt, art foam, or recycle existing flannel-board characters by adding a piece of Velcro hook. Flat puppets and props work best. Pieces that are too rounded will not hang properly.
• Attach a small piece of self-adhesive Velcro to each story piece so that it will stick to the apron.
• Place the manipulatives in the apron pockets with the picture side facing in. This will allow you to find the character you need quickly and easily.
• When you're ready to tell the story, invite the children to the story corner. Tell the children the name of the book and its author, and hold up the book so they can see it.
• After you've finished telling the story, make the book available for the children.

TELLING THE STORY
To use the story apron, you will need to stand and face the listeners so it can be seen. As you speak, turn your body slightly from side to side so all the children can view the manipulatives as they're added. As a character or prop is mentioned, remove it from the pocket, turn it to face the audience, and attach it to the apron. Characters may also be attached at the beginning of a story.

EXTENSIONS
1. After the story has been told, urge the children to ask questions about the story. The children may also want to create story characters of their own to place on the apron.
2. Ask the children to create their own story with pictures. Have them draw five to seven pictures that tell the story, or let them cut out pictures from magazines. Ask the children to tell their stories as they put the pictures in the proper sequence.
3. Stories that include colors, shapes, and numbers lend themselves to additional use of the apron for categorizing, matching, and sorting.

THE OLE STUBBORN PLANT
adapted by Mary Jo Huff

Once upon a day, a local farmer went to the store (insert the name of a store in your community) and bought some vegetable seeds. He plowed and tilled his garden until it was ready for planting. The farmer planted and tended the garden.

When it was time for the farmer to harvest his vegetables, he took a bucket to the garden and began pulling the vegetables out of the ground. The farmer took hold of the top of one **plant** and began to pull. He pulled and he pulled and he pulled, but that ole stubborn **plant** would not come out of the ground.

The farmer called to his wife to come and help him. The wife took hold of the farmer and the farmer took hold of the **plant** and they pulled and they pulled and they pulled. But that ole stubborn **plant** would not come out of the ground.

The wife called to her daughter to come and help. The daughter took hold of the wife, the wife took hold of the farmer, the farmer took hold of the **plant**, and all together they pulled and they pulled and they pulled. But that ole stubborn **plant** would not come out of the ground.

The daughter whistled for the dog and the dog came to help. The dog took hold of the daughter, the daughter took hold of the wife, the wife took hold of the farmer, the farmer took hold of the **plant**, and all together they pulled and they pulled and they pulled. But that ole stubborn **plant** would not come out of the ground.

The dog called to the cat to come and help. The cat took hold of the dog, the dog took hold of the daughter, the daughter took hold of the wife, the wife took hold of the farmer, the farmer took hold of the **plant**, and all together they pulled and they pulled and they pulled. But that ole stubborn **plant** would not come out of the ground.

The cat called to the mouse to come and help. The mouse took hold of the cat, the cat took hold of the dog, the dog took hold of the daughter, the daughter took hold of the wife, the wife took hold of the farmer, the farmer took hold of the **plant**, and all together they pulled and they pulled and they pulled. And that ole stubborn **plant** finally came out of the ground!

"Remember," said the little mouse, "you're never too small to help."

As you tell this story with the apron, place the figures so they hold on to each other. Saying that the farmer is trying to pull a plant out of the ground lets you create any vegetable prop that you like: turnip, beet, carrot, potato, etc.

STORY RETELLING

• When the children retell the story, let several of them act it out, placing their hands on each other's shoulders until the "mouse" takes hold and they all fall down.

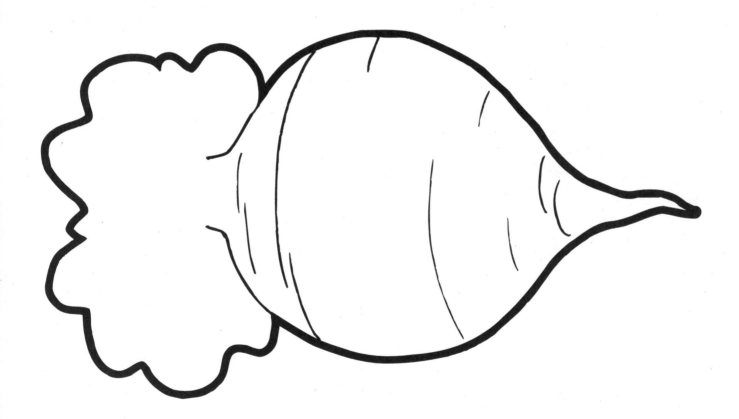

PATTERNS

WIFE

FARMER

PATTERNS

DOG

MOUSE

CAT

DAUGHTER

PORTABLE STORY BOARD

This Velcro story board can be used with a variety of tales. It can be held or set up on an easel and sized to fit your needs.

MATERIALS
Masonite or plywood cut to the desired size, Velcro fabric, scissors, heavy flannel fabric, sewing machine, needle and thread, wood for framing (optional)

DIRECTIONS
Cut a piece of Velcro fabric and a piece of flannel about 1/2" (1.5 cm) larger than the masonite; measure carefully so the fabric will fit tightly around the board. With right sides together (the soft side of the Velcro), stitch up three sides, leaving a short side open. Turn right side out. Insert the board and close the open end with hand stitching. Cut and add a frame if desired.

STORY RETELLING
The children will enjoy using these boards to retell old and new favorite tales. Stories that work well with story cans will also work with story boards.

FIVE LITTLE FISHES TALE

This tale needs only five fish and a whale for telling the story on a story board. The tale can also be told on a story glove, mitt, or apron, or, by adding a magnet to each character, on a story can.

MATERIALS
Paper
Markers
Velcro
Large empty coffee can
Scissors
Large paper plate
Glue
Brad
Paint (ocean blue and other colors)
Brush

DIRECTIONS
Fish—Cut out five fish shapes and color as desired. Give each fish a different eye color or shape. Glue on a piece of Velcro hook to the back of each fish.

Whale—Cut the paper plate in half. Cut out a tail shape and a mouth from one of the halves. Color as desired. Glue the tail to the other half plate and attach the mouth with the brad. Glue a piece of Velcro hook to the back of the whale.

Can—Paint the coffee can an ocean blue. Add drawings of fish, seaweed, and other ocean elements, if desired.

STORY RETELLING
The characters can be stored in the can and the story retold using the story board. The children will want to retell this simple counting tale again and again.

FIVE LITTLE FISHES TALE

Five little fishes heading for shore,
Along came a WHALE (gulp)
And then there were FOUR.

Four little fishes swimming in the sea,
Along came a WHALE (gulp)
And then there were THREE.

Three little fishes hiding from you,
Along came a WHALE (gulp)
And then there were TWO.

Two little fishes having some fun,
Along came a WHALE (gulp)
And then there was ONE.

One little fish swimming in the sun,
Along came a WHALE (gulp)
And then there was NONE.

PATTERNS

WHALE PUPPET

This whale puppet can gobble up the fish. His mouth opens very wide.

MATERIALS
Large paper plate
Crayons, markers, or paint
Glue
1 brad

DIRECTIONS
Cut the paper plate in half.
Cut a section of leftover plate for tail and glue to paper plate half.
Cut another section for mouth and attach mouth with brad for movement.

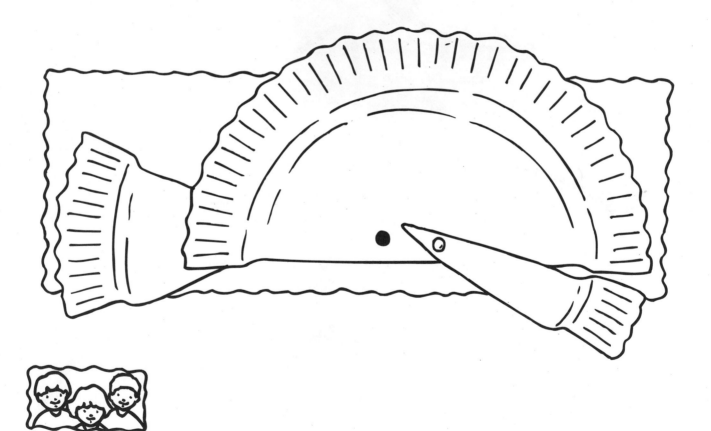

STORY RETELLING
Store the whales and fishes in a large coffee can that is painted like the ocean. Attach a magnet and Velcro hook to each fish and the story can be used in different story areas.

STORYTELLING VEST

Like the storytelling apron, the storytelling vest is worn during retelling, adding another fun dimension to story time.

MATERIALS
1 yard (.9 m) Velcro fabric
4 1/2 yards (4 m) colorful binding
Scissors
Thread
Sewing machine

DIRECTIONS
Cut out the vest following the pattern; the material listed is for a large vest and fits most adults. Place the sides together so the soft side is facing out and stitch across the top and down the straight sides. Serge the edges or sew on a colorful binding.

As you tell and retell the story, attach the characters to the vest as they enter the tale. Press the Velcro on the back of the characters into the front of the vest.

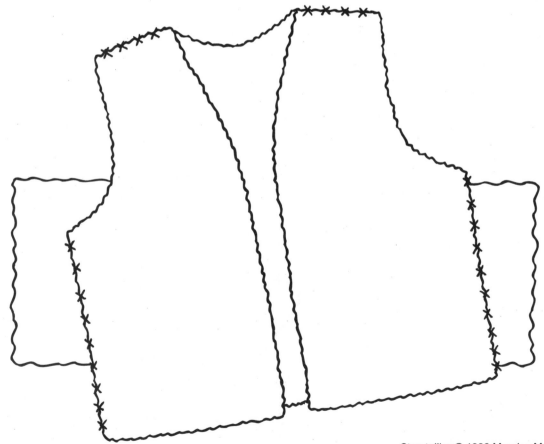

STORYTELLING AIDS

These storytelling props let the children be part of the story.

MITT AND GLOVE

MATERIALS
For each mitt or glove:
1/2 yard (.5 m) Velcro fabric
Fabric glue or thread and sewing machine
Scissors

DIRECTIONS
Following the pattern, cut material to the size you need. Place wrong sides together and stitch or glue.

STORY RETELLING
Children can wear the glove or mitt and attach story characters to them during retelling. Characters must be backed with a piece of Velcro hook to stick to the storytelling accessories. Stories with only two or three characters work best with these small surfaces. Gloves and mitts can also be placed in story boxes.

PATTERN

MITT

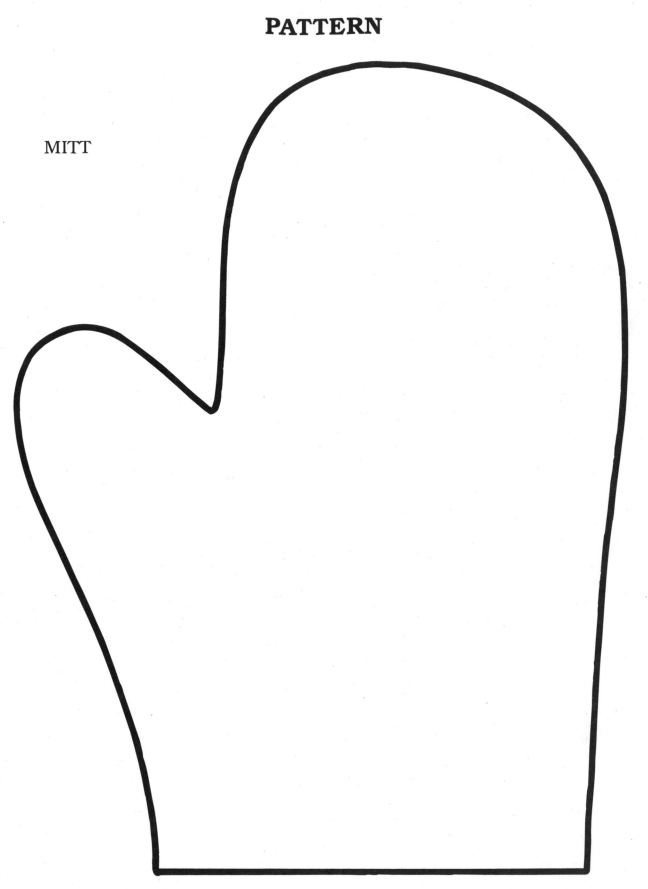

PATTERN

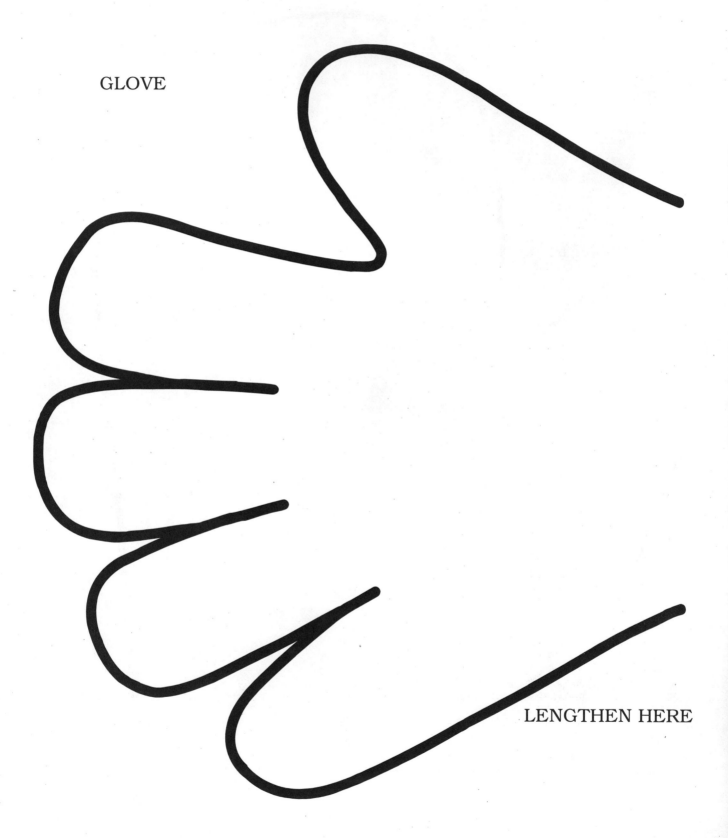

GLOVE

LENGTHEN HERE

HEADBAND

MATERIALS

1/2 yard (0.5 m) Velcro fabric cut into 2" (5 cm)-wide strips
Velcro hook
Scissors

DIRECTIONS

Cut a Velcro strip to size. Attach a piece of Velcro hook to the end on the inside of the fabric. This allows the headband to be adjusted to any size.

STORY RETELLING

The children can become part of the story they are retelling by attaching Velcro-backed characters to their headbands. Remind the children to attach only small characters and to place them so their sight is not blocked. Headbands can be stored by clipping them to string clotheslines strung across the story corner.

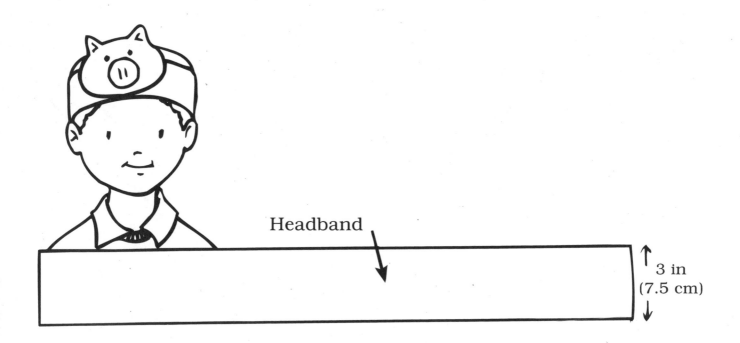

Headband

3 in
(7.5 cm)

STORYTELLING BOX

Story characters can be stored on the inside and stories can be told on the outside of this story box. Before you begin a story, ask the children what they think is inside the box.

MATERIALS
Cardboard box with lid (a copy-paper box works well)
Velcro fabric
Velcro hook
Glue
Scissors
Stapler
Paint and brush (optional)

DIRECTIONS
Cut the fabric to fit the box and glue it on with the soft side out. Staple the edges. Paint the lid or cover it with fabric. Attach a small piece of Velcro hook to the characters you will use to tell the story. The box can be designed to work with themes, such as holidays, seasons, farm animals, or fairy tales and for special holidays, such as Valentine's Day, Thanksgiving, or St. Patrick's Day.

STORY RETELLING
Place story characters, books, and props such as magic wands and headbands inside the box. Keep the box in the story corner and let children delight in retelling stories using the box's surface.

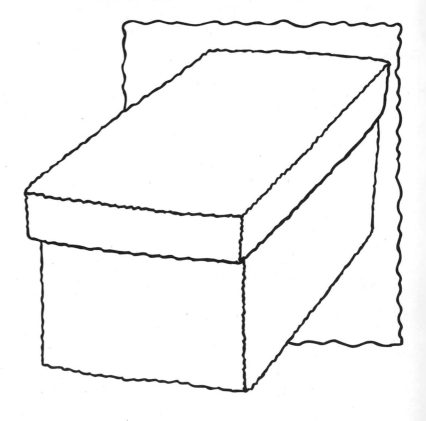

STORYTELLING CUBE

A soft three-dimensional cube invites children to sit down with it to retell a good tale.

MATERIALS
1 yard (.9 m) Velcro fabric
Scissors
Needle and thread
Sewing machine
Batting

DIRECTIONS
Cut out six pieces of material exactly the same size. Sew the pieces together with wrong sides together, leaving one seam open for stuffing. Turn inside out so the soft side is facing out. Stuff the cube firmly with quilt batting and sew closed the last seam.

STORY RETELLING
The children can use this cube by rotating it and placing characters on the sides, top, and bottom. Stories that can be retold well with a cube include "The Little Red Hen," "The Three Little Pigs," "Brown Bear, Brown Bear," and "I Went Walking."

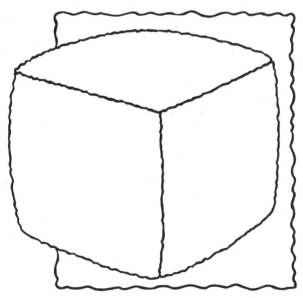

STORYTELLING CAN

Use the story can as a story center in which the children keep pictures that illustrate stories they've made up or like to retell.

MATERIALS
Empty coffee can
Spray paint
Laminator
Scissors
Old magazines
Paper
Markers or crayons

DIRECTIONS
Spray-paint the can. Let the children find pictures or draw pictures that illustrate a favorite story. Laminate the pictures and place them in the can.

STORY RETELLING
Keep the can in the story corner. Let the children reach into the can and share a story through their pictures.

STORYTELLING BAG

Before you start telling a story, let the children reach into this bag and try to guess what the story will be about.

MATERIALS
White pillowcase
Fabric crayons
Fabric paint
Iron
Ponytail scrunchy

DIRECTIONS
Choose a story and use the fabric crayons and paint to draw on a pillowcase design that illustrates the tale. Place items in the bag that will be visual aids for telling the story. Keep the bag closed with a ponytail scrunchy. A baby pillowcase can be used for young children or for stories with very few props.

STORY RETELLING
Put the story bag in the story corner for children to use in tale retelling. Keeping the story aids in the bag creates a sense of excitement and wonder.

Storytelling © 1998 Monday Morning Books, Inc.

STORYTELLING HELPERS

Storytellers often need help in getting ready to tell their stories, and in placing figures and props on storytelling surfaces. Children will love taking turns being the story helper, and you can make choosing helpers fair by using name cans to keep track of who has helped you.

MATERIALS
2 empty large coffee cans
Spray paint
Vinyl letters
Laminated paper
Permanent marker

DIRECTIONS
Spray-paint each can a different color. Use the vinyl letters to label one can "Story Helpers #1" and the other can "Story Helpers #2." Print each child's name on a piece of heavy laminated paper and put all the papers in can #1. Each time you need a story helper, draw a name from can #1 and then place it in can #2. When all the names have been chosen, start choosing names from can #2 and store them in can #1. The children will soon understand the process and figure out which can holds their name. If you like, let each child add a special sticker to his or her name card.

PUPPET STAGE

A portable puppet stage provides a special place for the children to tell stories and pretend with their puppets. While stages can be constructed, cardboard science display units that you decorate make excellent stages and are easy to obtain from most crafts or teacher supply stores. One unit can be used in the story corner or children can create individual stages to use on their own.

To use the display unit as a puppet stage, cut out a good-sized opening from the middle panel for the puppet to be seen through. Then decorate to suit a particular story, for example:

- sponge-paint a wild-animal or farm-animal scene
- stamp the child's hand print and add the child's name for use with a variety of stories
- paint on a flower garden
- use markers to make a space scene
- use watercolors for an ocean scene
- use crayons to create a circus
- glue on collage items

Set the three-sided unit on a table top when a puppet tale will be told, and fold for easy storage.

EXAMPLES

RESOURCES

STORYBOOKS FOR STORYTELLING

Alborough, Jez, *Watch Out! Big Bro's Coming* (Candlewick, 1997).
Allen, Pamela, *Who Sank the Boat?* (Coward, 1983).
Brett, Jan, *The Mitten* (Putnam, 1989).
Eastman, P. D., *Are You My Mother?* (Random House, 1960).
Fox, Mem, *Possum Magic* (Abingdon, 1987).
Fox, Mem, *Wilfrid Gordon McDonald Partridge* (Kane Miller, 1985).
Gliori, Debi, *A Present for Big Pig* (Walker Books, 1994).
Gray, Libba Moore, *Miss Tizzy* (Simon & Schuster, 1993).
Hutchins, Pat, *Rosie's Walk* (Macmillan, 1968).
Kasza, Keiko, *The Wolf's Chicken Stew* (Putnam's, 1987).
Lionni, Leo, *Little Blue and Little Yellow* (Astor-Honor, 1959).
MacDonald, Amy, *Little Beaver and the Echo* (Putnam, 1990).
Martin, Bill, *Brown Bear, Brown Bear* (Holt, 1983).
Pfister, Marcus, *Rainbow Fish* (North-South, 1992).
Shaw, Charles, *It Looked Like Spilt Milk* (Harper & Row, 1947).
Stevens, Janet, *Tops and Bottoms* (Harcourt, 1995).
Williams, Linda, *The Little Old Lady Who Wasn't Afraid of Anything* (Crowell, 1986).
Williams, Sue, *I Went Walking* (Harcourt, 1990).
Wood, Audrey, *The Napping House* (Harcourt, 1984).
Yolen, Jane, *Mouse's Birthday* (Putnam, 1993).

RESOURCES

STORYTELLING AIDS

Baltuck, Naomi, *Crazy Gibberish and Other Story Hour Stretches* (Linnet Books, 1993).

Bauer, Caroline Feller, *Handbook for Storytellers: With Stories, Poems, Magic, and More* (American Library Association, 1991).

Kinghorn, Harriet, *Every Child a Storyteller* (Teachers' Ideas, 1991).

MacDonald, Margaret Read, *Booksharing: 101 Programs to Use with Preschoolers* (Shoe String, 1991).

MacDonald, Margaret Read, *The Storyteller's Start-up Book* (August House, 1993).

Raines, Shirley and Canady, Robert, *Story Stretchers* (Gryphon, 1989).

Roberts, Lynda, *Mitt Magic* (Gryphon House, 1985).

Schramm, Toni A., *Puppet Plays* (Teachers' Ideas Press, 1993).

Van Schuyver, Jan, *Storytelling Made Easy with Puppets* (Oryx, 1993).

Vaughn, Gloria and Taylor, Frances S., *The Flannel Board Storybook* (Humanics Unlimited, 1986).

Wilmes, Liz and Dick, *Felt Board Fun* (Building Blocks, 1984).

For information on Varmint, contact:
> Playful Puppets
> 9002 Stoneleigh Ct.
> Fairfax, VA 22031

WORKSHOPS

For information on storytelling workshops, contact:
> Storytellin' Time
> 6722 Outer Lincoln Avenue
> Newburgh, IN 47630